Grief
for a
Season

Grief
for a
Season

MILDRED TENGBOM

BETHANY HOUSE PUBLISHERS
MINNEAPOLIS, MINNESOTA 55438
A Division of Bethany Fellowship, Inc.

Copyright © 1989
Mildred Tengbom
All Rights Reserved

Published by Bethany House Publishers
A Division of Bethany Fellowship, Inc.
6820 Auto Club Road, Minneapolis, Minnesota 55438

Printed in the United States of America

Library of Congress Cataloging-in-Publication Data

Tengbom, Mildred.
   Grief for a season.

    1. Consolation.   2. Bereavement—Religious aspects—Christianity.
3. Tengbom, Mildred.
I. Title.
BV4905.2.T47   1989   248.8'6   89
ISBN 1–55661–049–1

Mere presence of other people is not healing
in and of itself.
Rather it is the *quality* of those relationships
that facilitates healing.
—Robert R. Carkhuff

In tribute to Margaret Strickler ("Margy"), who often comforted me and many others, this little book is lovingly dedicated.

MILDRED TENGBOM was born in Minnesota but has lived much of her life overseas. After she was converted at the age of 15, she had to make a choice: follow her dream of a writing career or be fully committed to what God wanted her to do. She chose God's call to missions and went to the borders of Nepal. She also spent ten years in East Africa after marrying Dr. Luverne Tengbom. After returning to the U.S. she resumed her interest in writing and has authored 20 books. She is listed in *Personalities of the West and Midwest, Contemporary Authors* and *International Writers and Authors Who's Who*. The Tengboms recently served another term as missionaries in Singapore, but are once again home in the United States. They have four grown children.

Acknowledgments
and Thanks

I wish to thank all who from time to time during the past 15 years have helped me as I studied and thought about the subject of grief and bereavement.

To those who shared their journeys as we met in small groups or as we talked together or wrote to each other,

To the group of chaplains and pastors in St. Paul, Minn., who under the leadership of Rev. F. Larry Shostrom, Ph.D., Certified Supervisor of the Association of Clinical Pastoral Education, read the manuscript and offered helpful suggestions: Rev. Michael Dyrdal; Rev. William Ordermann; Rev. David L. Hunt; Chaplain Corinne Cavanagh; Sister Gerrie Lane, CSJ; Chaplain Bernd Soltau of West Germany; and Rev. Janet Warnes,

To Dr. Paul Wharton, Certified Member of the College of Chaplains of the American Protestant Hospital Association for 36 years and past president of the Protestant Chaplains Section of the Western Hospital Association,

To Rev. Paul Baglien, M.A., M.Div., fellow in the College of Chaplains, member of the Association of Clinical Pastoral Education, and trainer for Human Resources Development, for careful critique of the manuscript,

To William Backus, psychologist and ordained Lutheran minister as well as author of many books, including *Telling*

Yourself the Truth, for his review and endorsement,

To the authors of the many books that helped me in my own journey through bereavement and grief,

and especially to Sarah Ricketts, author of *Window on Eternity,* the biography of Jane Merchant (to be published by Abingdon Press in the summer of 1989), for allowing me to read her manuscript in which are contained so many of Jane Merchant's finest poems, and to Abingdon Press for graciously giving me permission to quote so many of these, my gratitude and thanks.

Contents

A Letter
From the Author

Dear Friend:

As I sit in my study, I wonder who you, my reader, will be. Quite likely you will be someone sorrowing because you have suffered a grievous loss.

This little book tells the story of dealing with death and grief. I chose to share mainly about my own grief over my mother's death. As Carlyle wrote, "A mother dead; it is an epoch for us all; and to each one of us it comes with a pungency as if peculiar, a look as of originality and singularity."

But it was not for this reason alone I chose to share with you my grief following Mother's death. While I felt the loss deeply, I thought it would not be as painful to read about as some other bereavements. I hope that as I trace my journey through this grief and as I refer briefly to others that preceded it, you may be able to relate your grief to mine—probably the sad parts at first, but in time the cheerful parts also.

Your loss quite likely has been different from mine. It might not even be the loss following the death of a loved one. Many losses are equally as painful as death. But the journey of recovery and faith is similar for all loss.

I send the manuscript on its way with some reluctance. I am sure that I shall never be through understanding all that God would have me grasp as I ponder this most sobering and profound of all human experiences. But I share what I do with the hope and prayer that it may be of some help to you, my reader. I pray that as you read, God will bring continued healing to you. May the grace of our Lord Jesus Christ, the love of God our Father, and the fellowship of the Holy Spirit be with you.

Mildred Tengbom

Before the beginning of years
There came to the making of man
Time, with a gift of tears.

Algernon Charles Swinburne

And I heard a loud voice from the throne saying,
"Now the dwelling of God is with men, and he will
. . . be their God. He will wipe every tear from their
eyes. There will be no more death or mourning or
crying or pain, for the old order of things has passed
away."

Rev. 21:3–4

Bearing Grief or Baring Grief

The crowd of passengers ahead of me and the upward slant of the carpeted ramp from Gate 51 of the Minneapolis airport slowed me down when I wanted to hurry. My gaze finally connected with the red-rimmed eyes of my brother Paul. I pushed through the crowds that had gathered to greet arriving family members or friends, and we stood, at last, facing each other, brother and sister.

We did not touch each other, because we knew that the touch of love would most surely cause our reservoirs of tears, filled to the brim, to overflow. Crying in public was not proper—or so we had been taught as children.

"You got the message?"

"What message?" I asked.

Paul averted his face. I saw his throat muscles contracting. Unsteadily, but determinedly he said, "Mother died at 10:48 this morning. She just slept away. So peaceful—like a wound-down clock that just stopped ticking."

An hour later I dragged myself into Mother's home and saw one of my other brothers standing, his arms extended. There, in the privacy of home, I walked into his arms. He held me close. Only then did I cry; we both cried. That release of tears was only the beginning of tears that would continue to fall for many years, often coming at unexpected times. But at that moment, all we thought of was how good it felt to cry. And so we cried. We all felt better for it.

Should we feel embarrassed about crying?

"He who conceals his grief finds no remedy for it," an old Turkish proverb says. Why, then, do we apologize when we cry? Perhaps we are afraid that if we cry people will think we're not trusting God, or that we're not strong or brave. We cry, however, not because we are weak, but because we are feeling the pain of separation, because we care deeply, because we've had the courage to love.

When Joseph overheard his brothers expressing their guilt for having sold him into slavery years earlier "he turned away from them and began to weep" (Gen. 42:24). Later, when he saw his brother Benjamin again, "Deeply moved at the sight of his brother, Joseph hurried out and looked for a place to weep" (Gen. 43:30). Some time later, when he finally was reunited with his father, Joseph "threw his arms around his father and wept for a long time" (Gen. 46:29).

The Lord Jesus wept over Jerusalem as He thought ahead to the suffering that was coming to the people. When He went to be with Mary and Martha after their brother Lazarus had died, ". . . Jesus saw her [Mary] weeping, and the Jews who had come along with her also weeping, he was deeply moved in spirit and troubled . . . and wept" (John 11:33–35).

Crying when we don't want to cry

A widow cries when the pastor announces a hymn her husband used to sing in the shower. Even the fragrance of a particular perfume, the smell of bread baking, the memorial service for another, a hug—any number of things can unexpectedly trigger tears.

What causes these unexpected outbursts? R. Scott Sullender, author of *Grief and Growth*, believes that we save our tears in an inner storehouse. Every time we hear, read, see or experience something that moves us deeply, we add to that supply. Finally

16

the storehouse gets full, and, when something even seemingly inconsequential touches us, the tears overflow, and we cry.[1]

The benefits of crying

In Joseph's reconciliation with his brothers and his reunion with his father, Joseph wept many times. We, too, shall have to empty ourselves of tears again and again.

When we cry, we experience relief—not just emotional release, but actual physical relief. Crying is our body's way of removing chemicals that build up during emotional stress, according to Gregg Levoy in an article in *Psychology Today*.[2]

He writes that the amount of manganese stored in the body affects our moods, and the body stores 30 times as much of the manganese in tears as it does in blood serum. A St. Paul biochemist and researcher, William Frey, says the lacrimal gland, which determines the flow of tears, concentrates and removes manganese from the body.

Frey has also identified three chemicals stored up by stress and released by crying: ACTH, a hormone, sends warning signals that stress is building. Scientists believe another chemical, Leucine-enkephaklin, affects the amount of pain we feel. However, prolactin, a hormone, comes to the rescue by stimulating tear production so the stress-stored chemicals and manganese can be released from the body, thus relieving stress.[3]

Experiments have shown women to have almost 60 percent more prolactin than men. This may explain, in part, why women cry about four times as frequently as men.[4]

Another study at the University of Pittsburgh School of Nursing has shown that healthy people cry more frequently and feel freer to cry than people who suffer from ulcers and colitis. Since both conditions are closely linked with stress, Frey suggests that tears might be a partial solution to relief of these

---

[1]R. Scott Sullender, *Grief and Growth* (Mahwah, N.J.: Paulist Press, 1985). Copyright, Paulist Press. Used by permission.
[2]Gregg Levoy, "Tears That Speak," *Psychology Today* (July/August, 1988), pp. 8, 10.
[3]Ibid.
[4]Ibid.

problems.[5] We need not feel ashamed or embarrassed for crying—it is both healthy and normal.

What if I can't cry?

Some people, however, *can't* cry, even when they wish they could. If we can't express our grief through tears, we can tell our friends how it is. It will help them understand why we are not crying.

William Stringfellow, in his book *A Simplicity of Faith*, related that for a full year following the death of his dear friend of 17 years, he did not cry.

At the same time, he recognized his need to be released from grief, so he would not, in his words, "become hostage to grief." He wrote:

> If I allowed this, the power of death would not only have claimed Anthony in the grave but would also seize me prematurely . . . I knew . . . the only way to articulate my love for Anthony would be in being freed from grief.[6]

But how was he to be freed? And why had he not cried?

First, Stringfellow had been ill. Business concerns, settling the affairs of his friend, and reordering his life had occupied his attention. But, he noted, "If my tears were yet constrained, it probably meant that my grief was still immature."[7]

The anniversary of Anthony's death found Stringfellow wandering the streets of New York where he had first met his friend. Suddenly he realized he was searching for Anthony. When he understood this, he said he quit searching. He went on to write:

> These matters . . . are not casual or insignificant; they are similar to those afflicting anyone seriously bereaved. What is involved in such issues is learning to respect the freedom of

---

[5]Ibid.
[6]William Stringfellow, *A Simplicity of Faith* (Nashville, Tenn.: Abingdon Press, 1982).
[7]Ibid.

the dead to be dead, honoring the dead in their status as dead people.[8]

Following this resolve, Stringfellow again found himself walking the streets, not searching now for someone he knew he could not find, but weeping because he had lost a dearly loved friend. He walked and walked. "I wept," he wrote. "I wailed. I gnashed teeth."[9]

Finally, as twilight approached, he walked through the open doors of a church where communion was being celebrated. He partook of the Eucharist. At the close of the meal, he wrote, his tears were done.

"But I don't like to cry!"

Many people—especially men—do not find relief in crying. They dislike intensely having red eyes and swollen features; they prefer to find other ways of venting their grief.

Some express their hurt from loss through anger—a method that is acceptable as long as we unleash it in a way that does not harm others. "I hung a punching bag from a tree in our back yard after Dad died," a young man said. "And oh, how I punched it!"

While crying is the usual way to relieve stress during grieving, there are always exceptions to the rule. We need, however, to find some way to uncork our grief in order to relieve stress rather than bottling it up inside.

The need for self-control

Although we acknowledge our need to express grief, we also need to evaluate when and before whom we should bare our grief. Are there times when we should silently bear it?

In a time of crisis, revealing all our feelings may be destructive. For in a crisis, we may act and speak as if we are immature people, untried in both faith and trust in God. Misunderstanding

---

[8]Ibid.
[9]Ibid.

may result, for few people understand that grievers must be allowed extreme oscillations in words and actions. Few understand that remarks made by one who is grieving should be balanced against the individual's character and demeanor under normal circumstances.

Maintaining self-control in public

One hospital chaplain has suggested that in order to maintain a measure of self-control over crying, some have found it helpful to choose a "safe" time and place to cry, a time when they are alone or with understanding family or friends. Some find an evening or weekend to be a good time to reserve several hours for deliberate, planned grieving. To get the grief going, he suggested that the mourners flood their thoughts with memories of the loved one: pictures, music, clothes, and perfume. Handle shoes that were molded to the feet of the love one. Deliberate grieving is a time to reminisce.

Active grieving at a chosen time and place may help to release tears, thus reducing the possibility of embarrassment by unexpected crying at inopportune times.

Balance in self-control

Certain other circumstances also call for self-control and restraint. Young children sometimes become very upset and frightened if their parents cry uncontrollably. Had Abraham allowed his son Isaac to see the fierce, wild struggle he undoubtedly went through the night before the two climbed Mount Moriah, the boy might not have been able to walk alongside his father in confidence and trust. There is a proper time for restraining emotion.

At the same time, we may hold back our tears in front of children when it would be wiser to let them see our grief. Parents' tears can give children permission to cry. Parents teach their children how to grieve for a loss by their own behavior. But parents usually over-protect their children, wanting to spare them the pain of facing death. The result is another generation of people who do not know how to grieve.

Children may interpret our lack of tears as not caring, and our times of tears as lack of control. Parents need to talk with their children and tell them how sad they feel. If we explain that we may cry from time to time, our children will understand that this is normal and will not worry about it.

One evening, a man told his children he was dying from cancer, and they all cried. Then they celebrated and had a barbecue because he was still alive. That evening, he said, the ribs had never smelled so good, and the stars had never shone so brightly.

Avoiding tranquilizers

Some people always will be uncomfortable when they see people cry. These dear people may urge a grieving friend to use tranquilizers. But such medications should be used only under a doctor's orders and supervision. Tranquilizers are habit-forming and can lead to far more intense distress than the pain of grief. There is no easy way "out" of grief. We can't avoid it. But we can bear it. God will give us strength.

> *O compassionate Savior, you are a Man of sorrows and acquainted with grief. I cry out to you in my loneliness. My tears have been my food day and night. But grant, O Savior, that my tears be not tears of bitterness, but tears of healing and cleansing. Gather up my tears. Put your arms around me and comfort me. May I know your presence with me. Even in my grieving may I bring glory to your name.*

I was there to hear your borning cry,
I'll be there when you are old.
I rejoiced the day you were baptized,
to see your life unfold.
I was there when you were but a child,
with a faith to suit you well;
In a blaze of light you wandered off
to find where demons dwell.

When you heard the wonder of the word
I was there to cheer you on;
You were raised to praise the living Lord,
to whom you now belong.
When you find someone to share your time
and you join your hearts as one,
I'll be there to make your verses rhyme
from dusk till rising sun.

In the middle ages of your life,
not too old, no longer young,
I'll be there to guide you through the night,
complete what I've begun.
When the evening gently closes in
and you shut your weary eyes,
I'll be there as I have always been
with just one more surprise.
I was there to hear your borning cry,
I'll be there when you are old,
I rejoiced the day you were baptized,
to see your life unfold.

John Ylvisaker[1]

[1]John Ylvisaker, "I was There To Hear Your Borning Cry." Used by permission of Lyons Management Systems, Minneapolis, Minn.

Presence

S unday morning, the day before Mother's memorial service, we faced whirling snow, numbing winds, blinding
sleet, and treacherously icy roads. But nothing could stop us.
We slid our way to the house of God. Our sore hearts needed
healing.

Stately Christmas trees stood resplendent with silver chris-
mons, richly symbolic in meaning; vivid red and white poin-
settias, huge evergreen wreaths, silver and gold garlands, and
bows adorned the sanctuary. I feasted my eyes on the beauty.
Strains from the four-console organ filled the sanctuary with
Bach and Christmas carols.

I saw the familiar faces of old neighbors, classmates from
long ago, a few new friends. Their eyes were compassionate,
their faces sober yet smiling a welcome.

God's familiar Word drenched my thirsty soul:

> The Spirit of the Sovereign Lord is upon me, because the
> Lord has anointed me to preach good news to the poor. He
> has sent me to bind up the brokenhearted . . . to comfort all
> who mourn, and provide for those who grieve in Zion—to
> bestow on them a crown of beauty instead of ashes, the oil of
> gladness instead of mourning, and a garment of praise instead
> of a spirit of despair. (Isa. 61:1–3)

The rhythmic, flowing melody of the ancient chorale enabled simple, homey words to crescendo into joyous praise. I joined my voice with those in the congregation.

O dearest Jesus, holy child,
Prepare a bed, soft, undefiled,
A holy shrine within my heart,
That you and I need never part.

I don't ever want to part from you, Lord! I love you. I need you.

My heart for very joy now leaps;
My voice no longer silence keeps,
I too must join the angel-throng
To sing with joy His cradle-song:

"Glory to God in highest heav'n
Who unto us His Son has giv'n."
With angels sing in pious mirth:
A glad new year to all the earth![2]

How can I feel joy at the same time that I am so sad, Lord?—But I do.

The invitation was given, and I knelt at the communion rail. "Take, eat; the body of Christ given for you. Take, drink; the blood of Christ shed for you." *I am so thirsty, Lord! As the hart longs for flowing streams, so longs my soul for you, O God! My soul thirsts for you, my living God. How present you are in your Supper, Lord! I need your presence with me, and I find it here.*

Then as the organist played the postlude, our friends gathered close, slipping their arms around my shoulders. Their hands clasped mine. "So good to have you home, Millie." Ah, yes, *I was glad when they said to me, Let us go to the house of the Lord.*

---

[2]Martin Luther, "From Heaven Above," *Lutheran Book of Worship* (Minneapolis, Minn.: Augsburg Fortress, 1978), used by permission.

Christ's presence in the personhood of others

Separation from our loved one causes us pain and anxiety. The presence of family and friends can relieve some of that pain. A friend whose husband had died suddenly said when I hugged her, "I needed to *feel* you."

Dietrich Bonhoeffer in his book *Life Together* wrote:

> The believer feels no shame when he yearns for the physical presence of other Christians. Man was created a body; the Son of God appeared on earth in the body; he was raised in the body . . . The believer lauds the Creator for the bodily presence of a brother. . . . Visitor and visited in loneliness recognize in each other the Christ who is present in the body; they receive and meet each other as one meets the Lord, in reverence, humility, and joy. They receive each other's benedictions as the benediction of the Lord Jesus Christ.[3]

Christ's presence in his Word and supper

Jesus understood the significance of presence. The day He bade farewell to His disciples, He promised them, "Surely I am with you always, to the very end of the age" (Matthew 28:20).

But how could He be present with them after He was gone? The disciples discovered that as they "devoted themselves to the apostles' teaching and to the fellowship, to the breaking of bread and to prayer" (Acts 2:42), they did experience Christ's presence with them.

Assurance of Christ's presence

When death separates us from our loved ones, we need the presence of friends and family. Even more, the knowledge that Jesus is with us can strengthen and help us. His presence often becomes real as we attend church regularly, partake of His supper, and take time to meditate on God's Word. We can pray,

[3]Dietrich Bonhoeffer, *Life Together* (San Francisco: Harper & Row, Publishers, Inc., 1954).

pour out our hearts to God, and let all our anguish spill out. His ear is open. He is listening.

When God seems absent

Sometimes, in spite of all our efforts to believe God is with us and to trust Him, we may find ourselves feeling abandoned by God. Jesus did. In His darkest hour He cried out, "My God, my God, why have you forsaken me?" And the Psalmist cried, "Why are you so far from saving me, so far from the words of my groaning? O my God, I cry out by day, but you do not answer, by night and am not silent" (Ps. 22:1–2).

We, too, may sometimes feel our cries are echoing in an empty room. Perhaps few pains are more distressing than the pain of feeling God is absent, the pain of being unable to believe in Him even though we want to.

When times like this come, we can learn from the discovery made by a woman whose boat capsized in a storm. As she was struggling to swim to shore, the waves submerged her again and again. A man on shore saw her and threw her a rope. Grasping it, she tried to pull herself to shore, but she was no longer young and had little strength. Sobbing, she gave up pulling—only to discover that her rescuer on shore had been pulling her to safety!

Jesus will do the same for us. He not only throws us a rope; but He pulls us in and rescues us too.

Faithful, caring God, I thank You that You have promised that You will never, never leave me nor forsake me. Help me to believe that You will see me through this time. I need you so much, Lord.

26

Death and the sun are not to be looked at steadily.

La Rouchefoucauld

The Season

*I*n the Midwest, the bereaved family schedules a *visitation* at the mortuary. People come, pay their respects to the one who has died, and express their condolences to the grieving family.

At the visitation for Mother, two voices inside me began to argue. *So why have we come?* one voice asked. *To view the art work of morticians and beauticians?*

Cut it out, Mildred! answered myself. *Don't be cynical.*

Well, what's the purpose of embalming, really? To cover up death? Make it look pretty? Death isn't pretty, you know. Death strips, impoverishes, causes muscles to sag, mouths to gape, unseeing eyes to remain open, facial expressions to go flat and dead.

I found a chair and sat down. I hadn't slept well for several nights and I was tired. *I'm too tired to think about these things,* I replied. *Besides, even I feel better seeing Mother—Mother's form— looking so peaceful. And don't forget,* I told myself, *many morticians are compassionate people who really care and want to help. Remember when that little Southeast Asian boy died? His mother wanted to spend the night with her dead son at the mortuary. I was taken aback by her request—it was almost a demand—but I promised I'd do what I could. The mortician not only agreed, he arranged everything—including blankets and pillows, as well as coffee, tea,*

29

and refreshments. "I don't know if the mother is thinking about the cost of the funeral yet," he said, "but please tell her there will be no charge at all for this." Remember that?

Yeah, that was one time, my other voice answered. *But what's the usual story? Why does it cost so much to die? Why do they run a video that features those caskets that are sealed tight so water won't get in? Why do they talk about some caskets having softer mattresses? What difference does it make, anyway? Why don't they show a simple pine casket that can be covered with a black or white pall? What do you think the markup is on the fancy ones? And why does it cost $80 to drive a limousine three or four miles? Tell me now!*

I sighed at my inward thoughts. *It isn't appropriate to think about money when one is burying a loved one, is it?*

That's exactly why morticians can charge outrageous prices, my alter ego continued. *Bereaved families are embarrassed to discuss cost.*

I shifted in my chair. *Oh, come off of it, will you? I agree with some of the things you say, but don't be cynical. And, now is not the time to discuss it. The first visitors are arriving. I must go to greet them.*

My brother Earl introduced me to some cousins I'd never met before. They were Catholic, and their conversation quickly told me that they had an intimate relationship with the Lord Jesus. We immediately felt close.

A young woman and her husband and two children stepped inside, stomping the snow off their boots. I recognized the woman to be the adult version of the blonde, pig-tailed, blue-eyed little Estonian girl who could remember only a refugee camp as home until she, with her mother, father, and brother, found a home in the empty farmhouse on my brother's farm adjacent to our home place. But as much as the house meant to them, even more important was the love and warmth they had found in Mother's home. Helle cried softly as she told how indebted she and her family were to Mother. Her family tried to comfort her. I was touched by her grief.

Mother's pastor had been moving quietly among the visitors. Despite the blizzard raging outside, 76 had gathered, some

30

from 50 or 60 miles away. The pastor called us to come together to the room where Mother's body was lying. "Let us have a brief service of Word and prayer," he said.

The grandchildren, in their teens and early 20s, had carefully avoided entering this room, but now they had no choice. They pulled chairs together in a circle in the very back of the room. The service began. Soon I saw their bodies hunched over, their heads bent and almost touching—a sort of football-like huddle. Their shoulders were rising and falling silently. Occasionally a loud sob from one of them intruded upon the pastor's quiet, measured words. The service was brief. Joyce, Earl's wife walked back to the little circle and began to massage tense shoulders. I followed. In the center of the circle on the floor, a little mountain of soggy white tissues was steadily growing.

"It's terrible to do this to a person!" one sobbed.

"Oh, no," I cried. "For everything there is a season, and a time for every matter under heaven: a time to be born, and a time to die; a time to plant, and a time to pluck up what is planted." *Dwight and Donald,* I thought, *you are farmers. You can understand this. Grandma did.*

"There's a time to weep, and a time to laugh; a time to mourn, and a time to dance. Yes," I told them, "times to mourn come too. And a time to embrace, and a time to refrain from embracing." *A time to run into the open arms of Carl in the privacy of a home,* I thought, *or not to touch Paul in the airport.*

They were all looking at me now. "And there's a time to keep silence, and a time to speak." *Thank God,* I prayed silently, *for friends who know the difference!*

The visitors left. We pulled on coats, boots, caps, scarves, and mittens; and with heads bent down, we stepped out to face the whirling snow.

Facing reality

Even if we have been present when our loved one died, after a day or two it's hard to believe it really has happened. Funerals help us look death in the face.

What if we can't view the body?

If our loved one died in an accident and the body was so mutilated it couldn't be viewed, or if the loved one died and was buried in a distant place and we, the survivors, couldn't attend the funeral, grasping the reality of death becomes even more difficult. Having someone recount the details of the death, or visiting the site where the death took place and being able to picture what happened, can help us accept that our loved one has died.

But even though I had been with Mother during her last days and had also attended her funeral, because I lived 2,000 miles away, once I returned home I could hardly believe her death had really happened. We had taken some pictures of Mother in the hospital. When we had them developed, I looked at them aghast and asked myself, *Did I realize how ill she was? Or didn't I want to know?*

Dealing with denial

All of us know how to practice denial without being taught—even Jesus' disciples were prone to it. Denial took many forms for them.

False optimism

When Jesus tried to forewarn them of His upcoming death, "Peter took Him [Jesus] aside and began to rebuke Him. 'Never, Lord!' he said. 'This shall never happen to you!' " (Matt. 16:22). Today's equivalent is false hope: "Of course, you're going to get better and come home. Those doctors have it all wrong."

Fear of the prognosis

The second time Jesus tried to prepare them, the disciples "were filled with grief" (Matt. 17:23). Mark adds, "They did not understand what he meant, *and they were afraid to ask him about it*" (Mark 9:32). We can understand that hesitancy, for we have wanted to ask the doctor questions, but we've been afraid because of what we might hear. Even when we do ask, we often refuse to accept the answer; as Luke said, the disciples "did not know what he was talking about" (Luke 18:34).

Concern over the inheritance

Mark recorded the unusual response of James, John, and their ambitious mother who asked that they be allowed to sit, one at Jesus' right hand and one at His left, when Jesus came to glory (Matt. 20:20–21; Mark 10:35ff). Their mother seemed oblivious to the pain ahead both for Jesus and her sons, so intent was she on getting the best portion of the inheritance for her sons. Patiently Jesus tried to jolt them into reality. He asked, "Are you able to drink the cup I drink?" Still they didn't catch on—or didn't want to.

Without question, denial seems to be an unavoidable component of every grief experience. And even though a visitation and funeral can help us face the reality of the loved one's death, still denial is a weed whose roots run underground and have a way of sprouting time and again.

Marks of denial

When we persist in denial, we may insist on keeping the clothes of our loved one. We won't change the room. One man told of how he continued calling home at noon even though he knew his wife wasn't there to answer. One bereaved wife continued to set two places at the table. Or we may deny the death by keeping busy. We fill our waking moments with TV or music—anything to distract us.

Sometimes our denial can be so complete we actually don't hear what is being said. Jean Sorenson of Seattle experienced denial when her husband Jack and she were told their eleven-year-old son, Bob, had a rare, incurable disease. As the months passed and his condition deteriorated, Bob seemed to know he would not recover. One day at lunch he unexpectedly said, "I know I am fighting for my life." Later, at dinner he said, "I think I am going to die in my sleep." Bob's grandmother distinctly recalled his words, but his mother Jean has never been able to remember them. She was trying to deny the reality of his impending death.

Other ways we try to escape the hurt

Sometimes we try to escape by identifying with that which is lost. A teenage son may attempt to carry on the responsibilities of a father who has died.

At other times, we try to soften the impact of the loss by forgetting all the hard-to-live-with characteristics our deceased loved one possessed. We insist on remembering only the good days prior to the painful loss—especially when the death has been a prolonged, distressful one.

We try to escape by transferring our love for our lost loved one to some other person, sometimes to such a degree that we almost smother that person. Or we may seek refuge from our pain by becoming almost childlike again, depending on others for even things we *could* do.

Necessary escape

We who grieve and those who support us should understand that we need some times of escape as a necessary part of the grieving process. When we are bereaved, we feel our loss has been too inconsolable to accept. We hurt too much. Denial and escape provide us short resting places, time to regain our courage and strength so we can go on.

How often we need to escape will vary with each individual. As time passes and we are able to remember our loved one with less pain, the necessity of escape will lessen also.

If too much time passes, and we still aren't facing reality, friends may try to help, and we may respond with resentment or anger. Sometimes others may know best when we need to get moving. Sometimes only we know when it's time to part with his or her clothes or make other breaks with the deceased.

In grieving, we just don't pass from one clearly defined stage to another: grieving isn't that orderly. Some mornings we may feel able to accept what has happened, but before noon we're plunged into despair again. Some have described grieving as going down a road that twists and turns, climbs hills, descends to valleys, and crosses rivers and plains. Others have compared bereavement to going through a long, dark tunnel. Whatever metaphor we use, let's remember it's important not to get stuck along the way.

Grieving is meant to be a *growing* process. According to an old Chinese proverb, we need not worry about going slowly, but we should be concerned if we aren't moving at all. So if we can't part with all the clothes, maybe we can give some of them away. If we can't change the room completely, maybe we can change some things.

Finally, if we're having trouble accepting the reality of the death of our loved one, perhaps we'll want to try saying the following words out loud, no matter how painful it seems:

"——— *is dead. Dead. Dead. I accept this death, Lord. Help me now to move on. Give me the courage and strength I need for Jesus' sake and His glory.*"

Unbelief is something very different from doubt. Unbelief is an attribute of the will and consists in a person's refusal to believe, that is, refusal to see one's own need, acknowledge one's helplessness, go to Jesus and speak candidly and confidently with Him about one's sin and one's distress.

Doubt, on the other hand, is anguish, a pain, a weakness, which at time affects our faith. We could call it faith-distress, faith-anguish, faith-suffering. Such faith-illness can be more or less painful and more or less protracted, like all other ailments. But if we can begin to look upon it as suffering which has been laid upon us, it will lose its sting of distress and confusion.

Faith-suffering is not as dangerous as we feel that it is. It is not harmful to faith nor to prayer. It does serve to render us helpless, and nothing so furthers our prayer life as the feeling of our own helplessness.

O. Hallesby[1]

[1] O. Hallesby, *Prayer* (Minneapolis, Minn.: Augsburg Publishing House).

Questions and Doubts

*I*t has to be here someplace, I thought. *I'm sure Mother said she was leaving instructions for her funeral. Ah, here it is!* In the top left drawer of her desk lay a small white envelope bearing familiar rounded handwriting. On the outside: "My last service on earth. May God watch over us all." And then underneath, "I wonder when you will open this." The paper of the envelope bubbled as my tears spilled over.

"She's chosen familiar hymns," I said to my brother Carl, who was to read the Scriptures at the funeral service. "But aside from the Twenty-third Psalm, the Scripture passages are Ephesians 1:3–23 and Philippians 2:1–11. Unusual, aren't they?"

Notes from my journal

> One A.M.
> Mother's home

It's no use; I can't sleep. The wind is howling around the corners, rattling the window panes. The house creaks dreadfully. I'm lying in Mother's bed, her blue electric blanket warming my body, but a chill deep within is keeping me awake.

I am unable to grasp—don't have the strength or courage to think about it, yet I wonder—where is Mother now? I have always said I believe in eternal life, but I'm not sure how to relate this to Mother now. I tried to express this to my family after the visitation today, when we were gathered around the table.

"Don't you agree," I began, trying to explain the questions that were torturing me, "that there's something totally baffling, overwhelming, profound, and mouth-stopping about looking at the corpse of one you've loved and known?"

Silence.

"When I looked at Mother's body, it was very clear to me that *she* was not there."

Lowered eyes stared at the table top.

I was persistent. "Then where is she? Why is Scripture so silent about this?"

"It isn't!" someone declared. "Jesus told the thief, 'Today thou shalt be with me in paradise.' "

"And where is that?" I asked.

Uneasy silence.

Then another spoke up. "But Mother herself told us that many years ago when she almost died following surgery, she had a vision of a place beautiful beyond human description. She said she heard music sweeter than any this earth can produce. And she felt no fear, no anxiety—only peace."

"I know. She often recounted the experience to me, too. It steadied her faith, helped her face death courageously. I don't want to discredit her experience, but, at the same time, isn't it risky to base our faith on human experience when it cannot be substantiated by the Word of God?"

"But we have a record of and witness to Christ's resurrection."

"Ah, and I do believe Christ rose from the dead. I believe He lives. I believe one day He will raise me—and Mother— from the dead."

I paused. *Did I really believe it?*

"I *believe* it," I said again, perhaps a bit too emphatically. "I can't prove it, but I have chosen to believe it." I drew a deep breath. *Lord, I believe, help my unbelief,* I cried out silently. *Better not to tell my family,* I thought, *but sometimes looking at a corpse sets even my faith in the resurrection quivering.*

"What is troubling me," I said, trying to get them back to

38

the question torturing me, "is, where is Mother now?"

"I think she's with the Lord!"

What does that mean, Lord? I think again now. *Where are you? Forgive me, Lord. I don't want to be a skeptic or sound presumptuous, it's just that these questions come!*

I crawled out of bed and moved over to the little rocking chair by the window. I breathed on the frosty window to make a little hole so I could peer out. A wintry moon boldly outlined the naked branches of the maple trees in the front yard. The wind whipped the snow into drifts and banks that formed intricate patterns on the lawn below. *Dwight will have to plow us out tomorrow morning,* I thought.

I turned from the window, slipped on my robe and slippers, and felt my way down the stairs. The stairs creaked under my weight. *Why do old houses creak so much?* I wondered.

In the living room I switched on a light. *Maybe my family in Anaheim, my dear husband and our children, will understand the questions that are tormenting me.* I began to write.

An hour later, shivering, back up the creaking stairs I went. How many grieving souls prowl around during the night?

Back in Mother's room, I closed the door and switched on the light. Mother's worn black Bible lay on the ledge above the bed. What was that passage in Ephesians Mother had chosen to be read at her funeral?

The passage was long, but I read it through until I came to chapter 1, verse 13:

> In him you also, who have heard the word of truth, the gospel of your salvation and have believed in him . . . were sealed with the promised Holy Spirit . . . which is the guarantee of our inheritance until we acquire possession of it.

Amazing words! The Holy Spirit himself is the guarantor of eternal life until we acquire possession of it. I had the Holy Spirit indwelling me—I *knew* that was true, for how else could I even have believed in Christ? That fact alone was enough to assure me of eternal life, that He will one day raise me from the dead. And if I believed that He can do that startling miracle, could I not trust Him to care for me—and Mother—until that day also?

I moved over to the little rocking chair by the window, pressed my face against the cold window pane, and peered out at the snow. *Dear God,* I asked, *can you still accept a child when that child doubts? My mind is up against a blank wall, God, but my heart is so hungry for you. I love you, Lord. And I do trust you.*

I glanced at my watch. 2:30 A.M. I moved over to the bed, crawled under the warm blankets, and turned off the light. *Tomorrow,* I thought, *we will lay Mother's body in that cold, cold ground.*

And what of my questions and doubts? I decided, as I pulled the blankets around my shoulders, that it would be wise for me to follow the advice I'd found in Jane Merchant's poem:

Today I close my door
And hope no one will come
Because I am too small
For anyone to see.

Sometimes flowers clench their petals,
Snails curve within sealed pearl,
Moles nudge deeper in darkness,
I close my door.

Hiding precedes revealing,
And smallness is for growing.
Tomorrow I will open
Many doors.[2]

And with that I fell asleep.

[2]"Today I Close My Door," from *Blessed Are You* by Jane Merchant, copyright 1970 by Abingdon Press. Used by permission of Abingdon Press.

In the long shadows of late November
we stood at the grave of one beloved
as husband, father, friend,
and I overheard soft-spoken words,
not meant for me,
but words to remember.

The moment had arrived,
that time that comes
in every hour of grief,
the moment for going on.
It was then that she,
the daughter and the only child,
spoke words intended just
for her mother, "Well, Mama?"

Two softly spoken words,
nothing more, and yet so much
in meaning and in courage,
much with which to turn together
toward a future with a different face,
words of hope and love, great love,
for we honor those who've taught us
to face forward by going on.

Gerhard Frost[1]

[1]Gerhard Frost, "Going On," *Blessed Is the Ordinary* (Winston Press, Inc., 1980). Used by permission.

Small Steps Toward Recovery

*M*y spirits lifted as we entered church, and I saw that it was as lovely as it had been on Sunday. "I saw the disappointment on your face Sunday morning when I announced that the Couples Club would meet Sunday afternoon to take down the decorations," Mother's pastor said. "We agreed to leave them up until after the service this afternoon." I squeezed his hand. Kindness comes in so many forms.

We filled two long pews: three sons and two daughters, with husbands and wives and seven of the fourteen grandchildren. I sat surrounded by my sisters and brothers, but longing intensely to have my own family, my husband and children, alongside me. I made some quick mental calculations. The plane fares would have been outrageous. I sighed and lamented the miles that separate.

Behind us sat aunts, uncles, cousins, neighbors, and friends. Some of my friends from missionary days in India and Africa had braved glassy highways and had driven from Minneapolis. I saw Mother's former pastor, Burdette Benson, and his wife, Elaine. Later I learned that they had returned late the night before from a long trip. Pastor Benson got the message this morning as he listened to his phone message recorder. He drove home immediately, picked up Elaine, and they slid the 200 miles to be with us. People care.

Strange, the thoughts that come. I found myself thinking of the taxi driver I talked to the last time I was in New York. An Indian, he had been in this country two and a half years. I asked if he liked the U.S. "If you have the money, you can buy anything you want," he had said, as we swung around a corner. Then he turned and looked at me. "But I cannot find love."

How blessed we are! I thought. *Lord, care for that taxi driver too*, I prayed silently. *Help him to find love.*

How strange, I thought, as I looked down the pew at my family, *we're all mourning the loss of the same person, but she meant something different to each individual, and the grief of each of us is unique.*

The service began with a hymn:

All the way my Savior leads me,
What have I to ask beside?
Can I doubt his tender mercy
Who through life has been my guide?

The music, the songs, the words of Scripture, the greetings, and tributes brought comfort. But most of all, I felt the comfort of the pastor's words: "A task remains for you," he said. "Reflect on those qualities in Mother's and Grandmother's life that you want to emulate."

Then he quoted Goethe, the German dramatist, who wrote in *Faust*: "What you have as heritage, take now as task, for thus you will make it your own."

"Do this," the pastor encouraged, "and then Mother and Grandmother will continue to live."

The sun filtered through the long stained glass windows and rested softly on our heads as the pastor pronounced the benediction. Because the weather was so cold, only the family would accompany the casket and the body to the cemetery, the pastor announced. When the family returned, friends could greet them at the reception.

In the foyer, as we again pulled on coats, boots, caps,

scarves, and mittens, memory suddenly thrust me back many, many years. I was a confused little girl who had slipped away from the family unnoticed and wandered back to the gravesite where men were nailing shut the box in which my beloved older sister, Amy, lay. With horror, I had watched them lower the box into the yawning hole, and listened to the plop, plop, plop of dirt as it hit the wooden box below. Terrified, I had stood transfixed.

Then someone had grabbed my hand. "Mimi, what are you doing here?" The hand pulled me away.

The memory of that June day—my birthday as well as my Mother's—crowded into my mind, and my throat constricted, threatening to stifle me. *God, how I hate interments! Do I have to go?*

A green nylon tent had been erected over the gravesite. We huddled together inside. The cold was penetrating, piercing, paralyzing.

"We're just family gathered here," the pastor said. "Why don't we take a few moments and share with each other something we remember about Mother and Grandmother?"

He looked my direction. Did he expect me to begin? I was caught off guard.

"I'm so cold, I don't know if I can talk without teeth chattering," I began, "but I know if Mother were here, she would say, 'Well, it surely isn't anything worth complaining about!' "

We laughed. The phrase was familiar.

I went on, "I remember the day we were going to take Mother to Disneyland. She hobbled stiffly down the stairs, clutching the railing. I could see her knees, swollen and red. 'Isn't the arthritis in your knees hurting you badly today, Mother?' I asked. She paused on the last step, drew herself erect, looked down at me with her faded hazel eyes and said, 'If you didn't ask me so many questions, I wouldn't have to tell you so many lies!' "

We chuckled. Earl recalled Mother's frugality, but noted how, once in a while, she would spend freely, justifying it by saying, "Well, we just have to have a little fun once in a while."

45

The phrase had become a byword for their family, he said, to resort to whenever they wanted a little fun.

We laughed again.

In a brief word of prayer, Mother's pastor gathered up the gratitude, love, and appreciation welling up within our hearts. As we walked away chatting and laughing, recalling other things Mother had said and done, I realized that the moments at the grave which I had feared so much, God had made light and easy—even joyful—for me to bear.

Grieving vs. mourning

Later I understood that I had begun that day to take the first tentative steps toward recovery. I had allowed the beauty of the sanctuary, the Christmas greenery, the stately architectural design that drew my eyes upward, and the gentle rays of the winter sun streaming through the stained glass windows to soothe my bruised soul. For the second time since Mother's death, I had permitted the organ music and the melodies and words of familiar hymns to speak to my heart. I had listened, really *listened*, to the Word of God, and it had steadied, calmed, and reassured me. Friends and family had gathered again to comfort me. And as I had recalled memories, I ventured to incorporate mourning into my grieving.

William Stringfellow, in his book *A Simplicity of Faith: My Experience in Mourning*, differentiates between grieving and mourning: "I understand grief, to be the total experience of loss: anger, outrage, fear, regret, melancholy, abandonment, temptation, bereftness, helplessness, and suffering privately within one's self."[2]

Mourning, he pointed out, has its root meaning in the Sanskrit word for "to remember." In Greek it is "to care." Stringfellow perceived mourning to be the reflecting one does about the life of the loved one. Gratitude, confession, intercession, and

---

[2]William Stringfellow, *A Simplicity of Faith* (Nashville, Tenn.: Abingdon Press, 1982).

46

resolution will result. Mourning can inject sweetness into the bitterness of grief.

Remember, remember

The Scriptures have much to say about memory and remembering in connection with death. "The memory of the righteous will be a blessing," Proverbs 10:7 says. Of the woman who anointed His feet with oil, Jesus said, "She has done a beautiful thing to me. . . . what she has done will also be told in memory of her" (Matt. 26:10, 13). When our Lord instituted the Last Supper, He told us to continue observing it in remembrance of Him and His death. And the Holy Spirit, Christ said, would call to the remembrance of the disciples all He had taught them (John 14:26).

An atmosphere for remembering

To recall and remember we need privacy and time to brood. "Forget about writing for a while," my husband Luverne advised me after Mother's death. "You need time to absorb and assimilate what has happened, to consider how it will affect your future."

We need an atmosphere of prayer and openness that will allow us to experience God's presence and permit His thoughts to flow into our minds.

What if we'd rather forget?

What do we do if we remember some negative characteristics of the deceased? We really don't want to talk about shortcomings, but no one is perfect. What shall we do with these memories?

It can be a growing experience for us to understand that if a certain characteristic of our deceased one irritated us, we likely possess at least a touch of that same characteristic, though we may manifest it in a different way. Our reflection about a deceased person may become a mirrored reflection of ourselves. If we welcome these new insights, we can deliberately seek to put aside in ourselves that which is not worthy.

Taking down the pedestal

By candidly identifying certain undesirable characteristics of our loved one, we are not dishonoring, but rather honoring our loved one. All of us are aware of aspects of our nature and behavior we wish we could change. The last thing we want is for our children or friends to become like us in certain respects: "Don't do what I do; do what I tell you." So when we remember with sorrow and repudiation certain aspects of our loved one's personality or life, we do not wound the memory. Rather, our loved one would approve and rejoice. Shakespeare reminded us:

> The web of our life is of a mingled yarn,
> good and ill together;
> our virtues would be proud
>   if our faults whipped them not;
> and our crimes would despair
>   if they were not cherished by our virtues.[3]

As we turn from the grave, leave the cemetery, and thus take our first faltering, trembling, uncertain steps toward a new life, we do not leave behind memories we have of our beloved. Rather, we let those memories stimulate and nourish our new growth, growth which is vital if we are to become more fully the persons God would have us be. As we do this, we shall begin to move from bitter grieving to bittersweet mourning, thus taking steps toward recovery.

More than memories

However, if the comfort of memories were all we could take with us as we turn from the grave, we might despair. But God's

---

[3]William Shakespeare, *All's Well that Ends Well*, Act IV, scene iii, 83.

Word has a far more hopeful comfort to offer us. As Martin Luther stated:

> We must henceforth learn a new language and speech in talking of death and the grave when we die. It should not be called dying but being sown for the coming summer and that the churchyard or burial mound is not a mound of dead bodies but an acre full of grain, called God's grain, which is to sprout again and to grow more beautifully than any can comprehend. This is not human and earthly language but divine and heavenly language. But although the world cannot speak or understand such language, we must learn so to use our tongue and to clear our eyes that we look at death and speak of it according to God's Word.[4]

Moving at our own pace

Let's remember also that immediately after the death of a loved one we may not be ready to receive the vehicles for healing that God has available for us. We may be so distracted we can't concentrate on God's Word. Doubts may torture us so we can't pray. Music seems to mock the awfulness of what has happened. To remember is the last thing we want to do; it's too painful. We need to be patient and gentle with ourselves, to give ourselves time. Even in nature some trees and flowers grow more slowly than others, but frequently the slow growers prove to be the sturdiest and most beautiful. Growth will come—in God's time.

---

[4]Martin Luther, *What Luther Says*, Ewald M. Plass, ed. (St. Louis, Mo.: Concordia Publishing House, 1987), vol. 1, p. 378.

And the Lord God made all kinds of trees grow out
of the ground—
trees that were pleasing to the eye
and good for food.
In the middle of the garden
were the tree of life
and the tree of the knowledge of good and evil.

Gen. 2:9

For the trumpet will sound,
the dead will be raised imperishable,
and we will be changed.
For the perishable must clothe itself with the imper-
ishable,
and the mortal with immortality.
When the perishable has been clothed with the im-
perishable,
and the mortal with immortality,
then the saying that is written will come true:
"Death has been swallowed up in victory."
"Where, O death, is your victory?
"Where, O death, is your sting?"
The sting *of* death *is sin,*
and the power of sin is the law.
But thanks be to God!
He gives us the victory through our Lord Jesus Christ.

1 Cor. 15:52–57

Death Is Not Natural!

I thought I had made a fair start toward recovery the day we walked away from Mother's grave; but once home, I found myself resenting that she had died. Death seemed so unnatural.

I had struggled to understand death years earlier, after the death of my father, then later when our two sons and also two dear friends died.

"Death is natural," some of my friends said. "Trees, flowers, plants—all of creation dies. We too are of the dust, and so we too die."

I found that response unsatisfying. *Weren't we created to live and not to die?* I asked. *How could God, after taking delight in the companions he had brought into being, want them to die? Would that not cause him sorrow also?*

God's first provision—eternal life

As I continued to struggle with this, I began to approach it from a different angle. In the beginning, God created Adam and Eve of the dust. They, like all other created things, eventually would return to dust. But God placed the Tree of Life in the

Garden so that as Adam and Eve ate of it as they were freely allowed, through God's provision their life would be constantly renewed.

The text: Will love be freely given?

However, at the same time, God recognized—I speak in human terms—that His relationship with Adam and Eve could be satisfying only as a relationship of love—and love is true only when it is freely given and when love prefers the other to one's own self. So God placed another tree, the Tree of the Knowledge of Good and Evil, in the garden. If they chose to eat of that tree, Adam and Eve would show their desire to serve their own interests rather than God's, even though they knew that choice would sever the relationship of love between God and them.

The mistaken choice

The garden home where Adam and Eve lived was lovely. All their needs were met. God was their daily companion. Sickness, pain, sorrow, and loss were unknown to them. Life offered them enough, but enough was not enough for Adam and Eve. They had to have more. They wanted control, power, and status. They wanted to be in charge of their own lives. They wanted to handle life on their own without God. And so they ate the fruit of the Tree of the Knowledge of Good and Evil. Instantly, their relationship with God changed.

Grieving over what had happened, God acted in a manner consistent with His nature. Fearing that they might take also of the Tree of Life and thus live forever in this broken relationship, God drove them from the garden and blocked the entrance so they could not enter.

Denied access to the Tree of Life, only one thing could happen to Adam and Eve. Created mortal out of the dust, they now would die and return to the dust. Although their death did not take place immediately, the slow process of decay did begin at once.

The remedy

Yet God yearned over them and longed for their companionship. Only He who had power over death was able to overcome death; and He accomplished this by sending His Son in the form of mortal flesh to die, bearing the penalty for our sins. Because His Son was part of God's own being, death would not be able to hold Him captive. He would live and, having broken the power of death by rising from the dead, would break the power death had over God's children.

We who name the name of Christ are still profoundly shocked when death confronts us, yet we can cherish the hope of life beyond with God. We still have to die, but now we can die with the hope and faith that God will not allow death to destroy us. Instead, God destroys death, and we rise to live again with Him.

How long a single night can be
We learned with anguished care.
Eternity was every hour
The night you entered there.

And even when the throbbing gold
Of day thrilled down the lawn,
We gazed with unfamiliar eyes,
Having no use for dawn.

Jane Merchant[1]

[1]Jane Merchant, "Eternity," unpublished.

The Odd Things I Do

When people react abnormally after loss, observers often say, "They're in shock." What is shock? Webster's New Collegiate Dictionary defines shock as a "sudden or violent disturbance in the mental or emotional faculties." In today's language, shock is the "double whammy" of any major loss, affecting us emotionally, physically, mentally, and spiritually.

The effects of shock

The senses

When I returned home after Mother's funeral, trees and flowers appeared drained of color. The songs of birds outside our windows fell flat on my ears. Food had lost its savor. My body felt numb and anesthetized, as though it had been molded of cement. To walk or move was an effort.

At other times I discovered my senses had been sharpened. I actually felt sharp pain in my chest, and my stomach knotted.

The mind

Some days as I tried to get a meal on the table, I found myself moving distractedly. I would partially set the table, mix half the orange juice, put coffee grounds into the coffee maker and forget the water. Sometimes dizziness caused me to grab for the counter. Once, when asked, I couldn't remember our telephone number. I was constantly mislaying my keys. I discovered the truth of Emerson's phrase, "Whirl is king." And I began to understand more fully why many counselors advise that survivors make no major decisions for at least six months after a major loss.

Sleep

Once again I found sleep evading me. Even when I fell asleep I would wake up tired, as though my brain hadn't been able to clear its circuits.

Outlook

People's laughter sounded hollow. I found myself remembering how after our second son died, I stood at the hospital window looking down at the people below, wondering how life could go on so normally. I was irritated—even angry—at people who seemed to carry on as though nothing had happened. Yet the rest of the world went about the business of life in normal routines.

Job's reaction

Perhaps few have described feelings as vividly—or as honestly—as the Old Testament character Job after he lost his family, property, and health.

"Why did I not perish at birth?" he asked. "For now . . . I would be asleep and at rest" (Job 3:11, 13). Instead he complained, "Nights of misery have been assigned to me. . . . When I lie down I think, 'How long before I get up?' The night drags on, and I toss till dawn" (7:3–4). Even when he did sleep, he was terrified by his dreams (7:14).

Job broke out with boils and sores (7:5). He developed bad

breath (19:17); he lost weight (19:20). He said his spirit was broken; his plans and dreams shattered (17:1, 11). His hope, he said, had been uprooted like a tree (19:10). He felt abandoned by God. "If only I knew where to find him!" he sighed (23:3).

Reactions to shock

Violence

One evening during dinner the phone rang. "Can you come immediately to Martin Luther Hospital?" The chaplain's voice was urgent.

He met me at the door of the emergency entrance. A friend's little boy had run out of the house and, without looking, had dashed into the street right into the path of a car. The impact had tossed him high in the air, and when he landed, his head hit the pavement with a thud.

I found the boy's mother sitting ramrod straight on the edge of a chair in a small private room off the emergency room. Terror had widened her eyes into huge brown pools.

A couple of hours later, after the child had been rushed to another hospital by an ambulance, a doctor broke the news as gently as he could. Her little boy was dead.

The news turned his mother into a wild, uncontrollable being. She pounded me. She scratched and bit my arms. She pulled her hair. She screamed. And she demanded to see her son.

In the emergency room she fell on his body, wailing, caressing, and holding him. When there was no response from his limp body, she threw herself onto the floor and began to bang her head. Fearful that she would injure herself, I dropped down beside her. At last, exhausted, she collapsed in my arms and buried her head in my breast as tremulous sobs shook her frail body.

Spiritual ecstasy

"I was carried on a cloud of joy and trust," said a friend whose husband had been killed when his plane plummeted to earth. "I didn't cry. I spoke of my joy in knowing that Joel was with the Lord. But," she added, "the day after the funeral, I crashed."

Seeming indifference

"The day Mother died I went shopping for new carpeting for our living room," one woman said. "I can't believe now that I did that, but I did." Often the shock of loss leaves us numb, unfeeling, unable to respond to what has happened.

Fear and dread

When my father died, I was just barely out of my teens and living in Los Angeles. I received word that a heart attack had landed Dad in the hospital. On the train back to St. Paul, I sat mile after mile with my forehead pressed against the cool window glass, my eyes staring unseeing at the landscape as it blurred past me. I felt as though I was standing on the edge of a deep, dark precipice, so deep I could not see the bottom. I was entering the unknown, and I was afraid.

People react differently to shock

Our reactions may be influenced by our loved one, our age, our financial status and health, the length of time our loved one was ill, whether the death was expected or unexpected. If we who are bereaved have skills in grieving or the capacity to develop them, we may react more positively to the shock of loss.

These all become important questions: Are there children to support? Do caring family members live nearby? Does the survivor belong to a supportive community? Was the bereaved's position, status, recognition, and identity dependent on the loved one who died? And finally, how strong is the individual's faith in God?

People who have faith in God are not exempt from suffering when they are bereaved. But they do have resources from which to draw. From the Scriptures, from prayer and worship, from the support of other believers, and directly from the Lord's presence, the believer in Christ has a vast supply of comfort and strength.

Help during the first stages of shock

A year ago, when I heard that my sister had died, I was alone in the hospital. The nursing staff asked if I wanted to lie down for a while. They elevated my legs and brought me a warm blanket. I assured them I was all right, but they insisted on bringing me a mug of steaming coffee. I called a friend to come and get me, and while I was waiting for her, one of the nurses sat with me.

At the loss of a loved one, we often experience some of the reactions I've described. When others can give the kind of helpful support the nurses gave me, they help reduce the immediate effects of shock.

Shutting out the pain

Perhaps no pain pierces and stabs more than the pain of separation when a loved one dies. We hurt so much we may be tempted to drown our misery by turning to alcohol or tranquilizers. If we find ourselves seemingly unable to cope without these, we need to find a family member, trusted friend, or pastor in whom we can confide, and ask him or her to find someone who can help us.

Better ways to cope

Sometimes all we need is support from those who love us. Trying to carry on as normally as possible and doing as much for ourselves as we can will help too. The days we make funeral arrangements will be busy, so we'll welcome the food and assistance neighbors and friends bring. But we shouldn't allow them to do everything for us or make all our decisions.

Sometimes the adult children of elderly parents want to take complete charge and make all the decisions. Grown children mistakenly think they are being helpful when they sell the home place, move the surviving parent to an apartment—sometimes in another city to be close to them—and dispose of all the clothes and belongings of the deceased. At times, of course, the health of the surviving parent makes these rapid changes necessary, but children need to be keenly aware of the multiple losses this forces upon the parent and do all they can to give support and care.

Generally speaking, as we adopt an attitude of wanting to care for ourselves as much as possible, we will discover hidden resources of courage, strength, and ability that will amaze us.

Most important of all, God is by our side to help us. "Do not fear," He says, "for I am with you; do not be dismayed [that is, do not lose your courage!], for I am your God. I will strengthen you and help you; I will uphold you with my righteous right hand" (Isa. 41:10). As we quiet our hearts, we hear Jesus saying to us, "I love you. I care for you. I will not leave you. I will be with you and help you."

Gracious, faithful, caring God, I choose to believe that you are with me now. Even if I haven't always given attention to you in the past, you have never given up on me. You have been with me all along, even when I haven't recognized it. But I need to know that you are with me now. Strengthen and help me. I feel so weak and confused and unsteady. Don't let all that I am feeling and experiencing overwhelm me. Put your loving arms around me, and carry my burden with me.

Full half a hundred times I've sobbed
I can't go on, I can't go on.
And yet, full half a hundred times
I've hushed my sobs and gone.

My answer, if you ask me how,
May seem presumptuously odd,
But I think that what kept going on
When I could not, was God.

Jane Merchant[1]

Weariness

8

*F*ollowing Mother's death, weariness became my frequent companion. I knew grieving was hard work. But what surprised me was how weary I was, and for how long that weariness carried on. Mother was 85 when she died. She had lived a full, rich, productive life. She had faced her mortality realistically but hopefully. She and I had talked from time to time about the inevitable fact of death happening to both of us, but more likely to her first. Somehow I had deceived myself into thinking my sorrow over losing her would not have as profound an effect on me as it did.

After Mother died I discovered once again that if I was able to drop off to sleep when I went to bed, I would awaken at 3 A.M. Many mornings I did not want to get up; I could easily—gladly—let the whole world go by while I just stayed in bed. I always did get up, of course, and forced myself to go through the motions of the required daily household tasks. But I could not write or concentrate; I felt dead inside. I wondered how those whose daily jobs forced them to continue could carry on, for by three or four in the afternoon I was often so weary that I had to lie down and rest.

As I turned to the Psalms for comfort, I found the psalmist putting my feelings into words. "I am like a desert owl, like an owl among the ruins. I lie awake" (Ps. 102:6–7). How I wished that I could say instead, "I lie down and sleep; I wake again, because the Lord sustains me" (Ps. 3:5).

When sleep evades

Like countless others, I tried many of the suggestions offered by books and friends. "Stop work an hour before going to bed," one person counseled. But I wasn't doing any more work than what was necessary to continue living, so that didn't help much. "Work on a puzzle, play board games," some suggested. Concentration, I discovered, was almost impossible. Still others thought crocheting, knitting, embroidering, or weaving would help. I had recognized the almost spontaneous urge to create something after losing a loved one, but only after several months had elapsed did my creative drive find an outlet in redecorating a room or working in our garden.

Music, I found, nurtured my battered soul.

Exercise helped. When sleep continued to evade me, my husband Luverne and I started to take long, brisk walks. These and swimming brought relief and a feeling of wellness. Sometimes after being in the pool, I actually felt energetic.

A few friends urged me to take sedatives, but I refused. I did *not* want to become addicted. Far better, I decided, to feel hollow-eyed for a while. If my doctor had prescribed sedatives, I might have listened, though I still may have been wary. Instead, I followed Dr. Glen W. Davidson's suggestion to eat something high in carbohydrates an hour and a half before going to bed. As the body digests the carbohydrates, it releases a natural sedative. According to Dr. Davidson's recommendation, I followed this procedure with a high protein breakfast.[2]

Sometimes when the hours of the night dragged endlessly, I would get up and read for an hour, drink a cup of hot milk, and then fall asleep soon after going back to bed.

---

[2]Glen W. Davidson, *Understanding Mourning* (Minneapolis, Minn.: Augsburg Publishing House, 1984).

Getting away from the noisy, crowded cement city and out to quiet places where my eyes could rest on views of mountains, lakes, meadows, and the vast ocean brought quietness and rest, and that, in turn, encouraged sleep to come.

Nature, however, can be both sweet and sour. Alvin N. Rogness in his book *The Word for Every Day*, refers to the sour aspect it held for him:

> It isn't true that nature is the healer. When in August 1960 our son was killed and could not join us at the lake, the pine and the birch which should have been the canopy for our tryst only haunted me with his absence. Something deeper than nature had to speak to my soul.
>
> It is nature's God who heals. While he reveals his majesty and power and order through nature, he reveals his love supremely in his Son, Jesus Christ. . . . To be sure, we can thank God for springtime and harvest, but to discover his love, we peer above and beyond nature to find a God who died on a cross for us.[3]

Thus, on those nights when sleep refused to come, I would recall a Bible verse and meditate on it word by word. An elderly friend told me he would go through the alphabet, thinking of verses that begin with each letter.

Praying for others was more difficult, but I tried that, too. Repeating to myself the words of hymns brought comfort, and reviewing the many specific instances when I had experienced God's help strengthened, calmed, and reassured me.

As weeks passed, slowly my old patterns of sleep began to return. Doctors have repeatedly pointed out the close connection between weariness and depression. As I slept better, I felt more cheerful, hopeful, and able to carry on. There were lapses in between, but those periods steadily became shorter. Like so many other unpleasant emotions and physical reactions that trouble us after bereavement, wakefulness and the resulting depression eased with the passage of time.

---

[3]Alvin N. Rogness, *The Word for Every Day* (Minneapolis, Minn.: Augsburg Publishing House, 1981).

You say you went back there? How did it look?
They've planted peach trees, as we wanted to,
Outside the kitchen windows, dammed the brook,
And screened the porch? I wonder how they knew
To do all that! We talked about it so
And planned just how to fix things when we could.
I guess they almost couldn't help but know
From living in the house. Well, well, that's good.
It's nice to know they've realized all our wishes.
I know that woman does her housework well
Looking at peach blooms while she dries her dishes.
I only hope they never have to sell.
Go look at it myself? Well, no. Somehow
I couldn't say good-bye again—not now.

Jane Merchant[1]

[1]Jane Merchant, "Home Place," from *Because It's Here* by Jane Merchant (Nashville, Tenn.: Abingdon Press). Copyright © 1970 by Jane Merchant. Used by permission of Abingdon Press.

Loss of a Home

That winter evening when Paul's car, bringing me from the airport, had crunched onto the snow-covered driveway of Mother's home, my face had been wet with tears. I wondered how I could ever get out of the car, or enter the doorway, void now of the welcoming presence of Mother. Her gray hair neatly combed and coiled in back, she would appear in a freshly ironed blue and white checked apron, bordered with white rickrack protecting a "second-best" dress, tears and smiles mingled on those soft, wrinkled cheeks.

That empty doorway—how I hated that doorway, never again to be filled with the presence of Mother! I remembered the anguished cry of our four-year-old Janet, years ago when we took off from the JFK airport in New York on the second leg of our journey to Africa: "Now I lose my home some more!"

Ah, yes, Janet, I cried silently that sad evening. *Now I lose mine! God,* I cried, *it's too much!* I've been a wanderer all my adult life, crisscrossing the U.S. as a teenager, traversing the sea to India in my 20s, settling briefly in Canada in my early 30s, only to leave and move our family to East Africa. We lived in Africa during my 30s and 40s, but returned to the States so my husband could do graduate work in Connecticut. At last we settled in California 2,000 miles away from mother, sister, brothers, and childhood home. Rootless—or rather, constantly uprooted, I knew only temporary homes. But I had found secure roots in this little white shingled house in the Minnesota countryside. Now, in a single blow, I was losing both home and Mother. *God, it's too much!*

Days later I was inside that little house again, sitting on the floor sorting through some of the items Mother had stored away. I heard the door open.

"Ann?"

"I've come to have a final walk through Grandma's house. I leave tomorrow."

Our eyes met in understanding. We blinked at each other. I got up. "I'll walk with you. We've different memories, you and I, but maybe we can relive them for each other. At least it'll help us remember."

Maybe, I thought, after Ann had gone and I had resumed my sorting, *maybe it will help if I pray for those who will call this house their home. Maybe that will ease the pain.* And so I prayed.

Other losses

The gray winter morning I drove out of the driveway of Mother's home for the last time, I wondered if with Mother's death I would "lose" my brothers and sister too. Mother had been the one to gather all of us home. If I were to maintain close relationships with my family and yet live 2,000 miles away, I would have to make a deliberate effort to keep in touch.

One of the men at church said that when his father died six months after his mother had passed away, their family fell apart. "The brothers and sisters never get together now," he said. "As long as our parents were living, all of us children covered up our differences in order to spare our parents pain. But after Mom's and Dad's deaths, I guess we saw no need to restrain feelings or words, and we found we were not only strangers to each other, but hostile adversaries."

Preventing further losses

Even though this man's experience hasn't been true of our family, the flame of love for one another easily grows dimmer and dimmer. Love needs to be nourished, and that requires effort and time. Often we are busy with other things that seem important—until death comes.

But time isn't the only problem. We also struggle with a hesitancy, an unfortunate reluctance to share our inmost thoughts and concerns with family. In Frederick Buechner's tale *Godric*, the title character returns home to find that his father has died. Of his father, Godric notes, "The sadness was I'd lost a father I had never fully found."[2]

Walls had gone up also between Godric and his brother and sister. So when his mother mumbles, "Your father lies beneath a stone," Godric thinks, "It's a stone as well we're all beneath. The stone is need and hurt and gall and tongue-tied longing, for that's the stone that kinship always bears, yet the loss of it would press more grievous still."[3]

Roger Rosenblatt, in his essay "The Freedom of the Damned," comments on the silence that imprisons families:

> Little murders are committed daily in homes where Mom and Dad sit planted in front of pieces of paper or *The Cosby Show*, while the children lie still as dolls on their beds and gaze at ceiling fixtures, like stations in a dream. See how free everybody is. The only things missing are the essentials: authority, responsibility, attention, and love. . . . Between parents and child there is no monster like silence. It grows faster than children, filling first a heart, then a house, then history. The freedom children seek is the *freedom from silence*. [Italics mine][4]

Not only children, but all of us, long for freedom from silence in our relationships with others. That silence can creep into our closest relationships if we are not vigilant and caring.

---

[2]Frederick Buechner, *Godric* (San Francisco: Harper & Row, Publishers, Inc., 1980).
[3]Ibid.
[4]Roger Rosenblatt, "The Freedom of the Damned," *Time* (Oct. 6, 1986).

Relationships can die before we do—especially relationships between brothers and sisters when they move away from home or when parents die.

Loss of home

Those who lose a spouse through death sometimes have to move to a smaller home or even to a different city, either for financial reasons or to be nearer relatives. When they do so, they also experience the loss of a home. Such uprooting brings a double bereavement, the loss of two familiar and loving "family members."

Older people who have to move into health care centers may suddenly find themselves sharing a room with a stranger. When they must part with their possessions, keeping only the essentials, small and fewer treasures become even more cherished. Jane Merchant, whose parents had to move to smaller and smaller homes because of financial constraints imposed by illness and death, knew what such losses were like. She wrote of the comfort she derived from keeping a little Dutch-girl pitcher and a tiny Chinese gentleman whose quaint expression used to stop her quick tears when she was a child.

Making transitions

The pain of saying farewell to one home and entering another may be softened by an informal service. One pastor said, "I have had prayer and a service of benediction in the home that is being left, and then have gone with the person to the nursing home and repeated the same ritual. Always, the person moving has expressed appreciation, sometimes with tears."

The use of music, words, and movement—walking out of one home and into another—charge a service with meaning. Words should be comforting and reassuring, words with promises of hope for tomorrow but also acknowledgments of the hurt and loss.

The same ceremony can be used when the surviving family

members gather to decide to whom the clothes and other personal belongings should be given. Memories associated with possessions can be shared, and then prayer is offered: prayers of thanksgiving for the one who used the goods and the happy times associated with the articles, and prayers of intercession for those who will receive the gifts. Some families like to sing as the boxes are carried from the home. Practicing such rituals over and over can give the family a sense of identity, continuity, and security.

God's constancy

Emptying a house may be a sad event, but prayer can assuage the hurt. The "stone that lies over us as kin" may seem heavy, preventing us from reaching out to embrace each other with shared thought, forgiveness, and open hearts. But God is able to roll away that stone too. He can resurrect new warmth and deepened, compassionate understanding in our family members who remain. He also can give us courage to move to new communities, ease the pain of simplifying our material lives, and help us reach out to find new friends. And if the pain of moving impresses on us that here "we have no abiding city," the loss of home will prove eminently worthwhile.

Just what he had against it I can't say.
It was a harmless-looking box enough
That he was treating in a shameful way,
Kicking it ahead of him with rough
Enthusiastic kicks, with such a fierce
Impetuous joy, it seemed as if his toe
Was surely bound, with each kick, to pierce
Right through the cardboard side. It didn't though,
And he kept kicking at it out of sight
And getting happier with every kick
Like all of us who watched him with delight.
We'd been hurt too. We'd been hurt to the quick,
And we were eased of angers and of shocks
By every kick he gave that empty box.

Jane Merchant[1]

---

[1]Jane Merchant, "Boy Kicking Box," from *Halfway up the Sky* (Nashville, Tenn.: Abingdon Press). Copyright renewal © 1985 by Elizabeth Merchant. Used by permission of Abingdon Press.

Irritable Days

As we grieve, sooner or later we may feel anger boiling up; most people feel angry when someone or something they love is snatched from them.

My journal:

January 21

I so often feel irritated and impatient these days, and I have trouble treating Luverne with gentleness, courtesy, and consideration. I have wondered why. I mentioned it to a friend, and she suggested that maybe one reason for my feeling so crabby was anger—anger at death itself.

Sometimes anger can produce good results. Mothers whose children were killed by drunken drivers organized MADD to get drunk drivers off the streets. Their anger was channeled into a positive force. But resentment and anger can also be treacherous and destructive emotions. To deal properly with anger, we need to recognize we are only imperfect human beings, and so we get angry. We confess our anger. And then we seek God's help to overcome it.

Why we get angry

Gerhard Frost said of his golden retriever, "She's fiercest when she's most afraid." For us, as well, anger is often a cover-up emotion. When we feel guilty, insecure, lonely, abandoned, or betrayed, we often express those feelings through anger. Hurt usually lies behind anger, hidden emotions we may not be consciously aware of, but feelings that nevertheless influence our attitudes and actions toward those around us.

We feel mistreated

Often in our anger, we may think the doctor, the nurses, or the hospital didn't give our loved one proper care. "I not only think so," one man insisted, "I *know* so." Perhaps our pastor or the hospital chaplain didn't visit frequently enough, or the paramedics didn't sound the siren when they drove our injured loved one to the hospital. We always can find someone to blame for our loss. In extreme cases, we may feel no one treated us right.

We feel God let us down

Job was angry at God because he felt God had treated him unfairly. "Why do the wicked live on, growing old and increasing in power?" he asked. "They see their children established around them, their offspring before their eyes" (Job 21:7–8). He elaborated on their lack of regard for God, then asked bitterly, "How often does calamity come upon them, the fate God allots in his anger?" (Job 21:17). "It isn't fair!" Job was saying.

No, Job, it isn't fair. Life isn't fair.

Our first son was born prematurely and lived only a few hours. When a year later, our second premature son died, I felt I had been treated unjustly. *It's not fair!* I stormed. *Thousands of women thoughtlessly or carelessly conceive children only to destroy them.* We would cherish, love and do all we could to be good parents, and we were being denied children.

We feel helpless

My doctor, committed to prolonging life, felt helpless when our two babies died, and he vented his helplessness in angry

74

words. Acute feelings of helplessness and anger can almost overwhelm widows and widowers after the death of a spouse. One widower had never realized how much his wife had done for him until after she had died. He discovered then that he didn't know how to cook; he didn't know where his wife kept things; he couldn't operate a washer or dryer. His wife also had handled all the family's finances and records. He was ashamed to admit it, but he didn't know how to make out an income tax form. He *did* know how to handle his own business well. In fact, he realized too late that because he had devoted so much time to his business, he knew little about his family's affairs.

"Maybe I'm partly to blame," he admitted, but then quickly flared, "but I'm still mad at my wife. Why didn't she insist that I learn? Why did she *die?*"

We feel unappreciated

Survivors who have cared for ailing loved ones and discover they have not been remembered adequately in the will may feel betrayed. They struggle with feelings of resentment.

Job felt God had betrayed him. He had been righteous before God, so why were all these bad things happening to him?

"Why have you made me your target?" Job asked bitterly. His understanding of God's character had become so distorted that he began to say terrible things about God, implying that God was unjust and cruel. "Even if I washed myself with soap and my hands in washing soda, you would plunge me into a slime pit so that even my clothes would detest me," he protested (Job 9:30). Job accused God of being deceitful. "But this is what you concealed in your heart, and I know that this was in your mind," he said (Job 10:13).

For finger-shaking, foot-stamping, name-calling expressions of anger, few of us have surpassed brother Job. And God listened quietly until Job began to move so far away from reality that he was in danger of falling into serious error. Then God stepped in and confronted him, and Job had to deal with his anger.

In every relationship, certain characteristics of our beloved irritate us. Strangely enough, memories of these irritations often have a way of surfacing after the person's death, and we find ourselves angry again. If we learned how to handle those irritations while our loved ones were living and our fickle emotions are returning now just to make us miserable, we can treat the whole matter as "old business," already settled. We can refuse to brood over negative feelings that pop up. If we've never dealt with our resentments, we can take them to the Lord, receive His forgiveness, and be set free.

Sometimes someone else has hurt us—someone completely separate from the loved one who has died. But we have not dealt with the hurt we felt from that incident. The anger we normally feel at being bereaved joins forces with the previous unresolved anger and heats up almost to the point of rage.

If our anger seems excessive, and if we don't really know why we're so angry, perhaps we need to consider previous painful experiences and seek healing for those old hurts.

We may feel angry at those who do not seem to understand us, those who are not hurting as we are. Or we may just feel angry at life in general and cast about for someone to blame.

Leonore Lowry, in writing about the death of her three-year-old son Stephen, noted, "I struggled with feelings of rejection toward my remaining four lively, healthy, children." In such cases, support groups can be very helpful.

Venting anger

We can dispel our anger by going for a long walk, hitting a punching bag, shoveling snow, swimming—any exercise may help. A middle-aged wife said that when her husband became seriously ill, she would hack away at a tree stump they had in their back yard. As the chips of wood flew, her anger and stress would fly away with the chips.

We need to guard against venting our anger on innocent

parties, those we care for most, those who are puzzled by our outbursts. Rather than accusing others for making us angry, we need to learn to say "I feel angry" and thus take responsibility for our anger.

Better yet, if we must voice our anger, we can find a neutral person who can listen objectively—a counselor, pastor, or other professional. Some people have difficulty listening to angry people, and relationships may suffer damage as we work through our anger.

Job's friends not only felt uncomfortable, they were horrified when Job started to unleash his anger against God. Not knowing how to deal with him, they confronted Job with condemnation. "When your children sinned against God, he gave them over to the penalty of their sin," they insisted (Job 8:4). In other words, "They got what they deserved; shut up, Job." That sort of talk helped neither Job nor his relationship with his friends.

Supporting an angry griever

When a grieving friend unloads anger, we can best help by listening quietly and trying to understand where the real hurt lies. Is the person blaming himself, even though he is unaware of doing so? Is his guilt being vented in anger and targeted at innocent parties?

And if grieving family members vent their anger at us, and we are innocent, we do not have to take their anger personally. We can ask God to help us to listen and turn that anger over to God.

"But I think my sister always felt bitter toward me but never expressed it before," one woman said. "I think that Father's death just revealed her for what she really was."

Perhaps the woman was right in her evaluation. But even if bereavement does unclothe undesirable traits, we can accept the individuals as they are without condoning their behavior. Rather than focusing on the negative characteristics, we can pray and believe that change will come, that the person will become a better individual because of all that has happened.

Goethe wrote: "If we treat people as if they were what they ought to be, we help them become what they are capable of becoming."

The Christlike response to anger

While John's wife Marge lay dying of cancer in the hospital, a woman whose husband was recovering from surgery popped in to see Marge daily, often bringing along her visitors. As Marge lay with eyes closed, the woman would whisper, "Look at what cancer does! Skin and bones. Gosh, how her cheek bones protrude! But look at the edema. See her elbows? And her feet!" Gingerly she would lift up a corner of the sheet. "Elephant feet, aren't they? Her belly is beginning to swell, too. Awful, Judy, awful!"

"I was ready to haul off and sock her," John admitted, but after she had left the room Marge would open her eyes and calm me down by saying, 'Let's pray for her, dear. Something's eating her.' "

As the days passed, John learned the woman's husband's surgery had uncovered cancer that had spread throughout his organs.

"She can't accept it. She's denying it. We have to be patient," Marge said to John when the visits and the remarks continued.

Finally, the doctors sent the man home. A few days later Marge died. John's home echoed with loneliness, a loneliness he knew would not disappear on its own. As he prayed for guidance, only one thought came to mind: *Visit that man who has cancer.*

As he did, John discovered the man liked a special kind of bread. John searched till he found a store that sold it. The man used to enjoy camping, so John brought slides of camping trips.

One night, while John was projecting the slides on the bed-side wall, his friend fell asleep. John switched off the projector. An hour later when the man awoke and saw John still sitting there, he quickly turned his head to the wall. When he looked at John again, his face was wet with tears.

"Why do you care for me?" he asked.

"Because I know how much Christ cares for me," John said simply.

Increasing weakness sent John's friend back to the hospital. Daily John went to see him. When the doctor once again sent him home, John drove the ten miles to visit him.

One day John's pastor received a phone call. The man on the line explained who he was, and then said, "I want to be baptized." John was glad he had learned to see beyond the rude remarks made by the man's wife in the hospital and that he had been faithful to show love to this dying friend.

"Never let anger control you," Chinese philosopher Meng-Tse admonishes. "Otherwise, in one day, you could burn up the wood you collected in many bitter weeks."[2]

"Be angry but sin not," Scripture commands (Eph. 4:26). With God's help we can understand why we are angry, confess it, learn to express it in ways that won't hurt others or ourselves, and seek God's help to overcome it.

[2]*Springs of Chinese Wisdom* (New York: Herder & Herder Publishers, 1971).

How long, O Lord? Will you forget me forever?
How long will you hide your face from me?
How long must I wrestle with my thoughts
and every day have sorrow in my heart?
How long will my enemy triumph over me?

Look on me and answer, O Lord my God,
Give light to my eyes, or I will sleep in death;
my enemy will say, "I have overcome him,"
and my foes will rejoice when I fall.

But I trust in your unfailing love;
my heart rejoices in your salvation.
I will sing to the Lord,
for he has been good to me.

Ps. 13:1–6

Emotions and Faith

*M*y journal:

January 19

Thursday the fact of Mother's death began to take on a certain sense of unreality. Thursday and Friday were hard days with feelings of depression and deep sadness.

January 31

"It was now dark, but Jesus had not yet come to them" (John 6:17).

Why does the physical darkness of the night accentuate the darkness of the soul? That darkness deepens when the individuals are not conscious of the presence of the Lord with them. What a dilemma the disciples faced. In the dark, alone in a little fishing boat on the Sea of Galilee; that unpredictable and treacherous sea. And Jesus—who knows where He has gone? I feel with the disciples their anxiety, their confusion, possibly even their resentment.

"He had not yet come to them." Does this imply that they were expecting Him to come? Or is the storyteller, who knows how the story ends, making this statement?

Is my situation that of Jesus not having come to me yet? Hang on, Millie. The condition must worsen before He will come. "The sea rose because a strong wind was blowing."

Only when the condition has become so desperate that the disciples fear for survival, when they know they cannot make it on their own—only then does Jesus come.

But isn't the night already dark enough for me, Lord? Why does it have to get darker? Won't you come to me through the dark, across the waters? Come, Lord Jesus, oh, come!

February 10

"None of these things move me," Paul wrote. Not, "None of these things distress me," or "hurt me," but "None of these things *move* me." I anchor my trust in Jesus regardless of how I feel. It's good I can do this, because I feel so depressed.

March 4

Dave called last night—crying, actually crying. Exactly a year ago, his fiancee was killed in a tragic automobile accident and he was so maimed he was no longer able to work. Such anniversaries are always tough, so I'd sent a card.

"It's so hard, Millie," he said. "Physically I still hurt all over. It's hard to be alive like this. I manage the housework— that's about all. Time is endless."

"Others have told me that deliberately praising God helps rescue them," I ventured carefully. "Do you sing, Dave?"

"Like a crow!" He actually managed a laugh between his sobs.

"Never mind. No one'll hear you. Why don't you try that, huh?" *You too, Millie,* I heard the Lord say.

"Forgive me, Millie. Sometimes I start to slide down into that mucky little trough of self-pity. I *do* have much to be thankful for. Friends. Church. Music. Books."

"It's hard not to feel sorry for ourselves," I said. "Sometimes it almost makes us feel good." I thought I heard a feeble laugh.

"I get so angry at that crazy, drunken fool who wrecked our lives! I sometimes think I've dealt with it, and then it pops up again."

Long ago I heard Corrie ten Boom tell of the struggle she had forgiving those who had imprisoned and abused both her sister and her during World War II. She would think she had forgiven them, and then something would happen to cause anger to flare again.

Finally, she went to her pastor.

"Corrie," he said, "you're familiar with our church bell, aren't you?"

She nodded.

"Have you noticed what happens when our sexton stops ringing it? It continues going ding . . . dong, ding . . . dong, but the space between the ding-dongs gets longer and longer. It'll be that way for you too, Corrie. As you continue asserting your forgiveness, the resentment gradually will surface less and less frequently."

I related the story to Dave. Only silence answered me for a moment. Then he said softly, "Thank you, Millie."

Jesus, I prayed after we both had hung up, *meet Dave's need. You've met them before. Do it again.*

April 18

I read Romans 12:2 this morning. "Be not conformed to this world, but be transformed by the renewing of your mind." The renewing of my mind—what does that mean? Deliberately shifting my focus from myself and my sorrows to others? Staying my faith on what God has declared? Consoling my heart with the psalmist's cries of anguish, and embracing the psalmist's statements of trust and hope?

Faith and hope

My feelings of depression after Mother's death were not as severe as they were when our babies died. At that time, I had felt I'd been betrayed, let down. I'd hoped in God in vain. *I don't want to give up on God completely,* I said to myself, *but I'm not sure just how much I'll ever ask of Him again.*

Immediately after the death of our second tiny son I didn't even want to live. I'd been running a fever; they couldn't identify the reason, and medication wasn't bringing it down. One day my doctor came to talk to me. I still can't remember what he said, but he made me so mad! That night, my temperature went down and never climbed again.

After getting angry, I started to want to live again. The day my doctor told me I could go home, he smiled. "Sorry I had to say to you what I did," he apologized, "but I had to do something to get you to fight back."

When I went for a check-up, *he* was angry things had gone as they had. He flung his gloves in the sink; the water and soapsuds flew as he scrubbed his hands and fumed because our babies hadn't lived. I felt *so good* that he was mad. His anger gave me permission to be mad. If I could have expressed my anger instead of keeping quiet about it like a "good Christian," I would have made a more complete emotional and spiritual recovery at an earlier date.

It took time for me to comprehend that all trust is haunted by some doubt. It's risky petitioning God, because inherent in every request is the possibility of failure. Faith carries a certain amount of risk.

That's why faith calls for courage. Ruth the Moabitess exhibited that faith and courage. When her father-in-law and her husband died, she chose to leave all that represented security— her family, friends, and country—to go with her mother-in-law Naomi as Naomi returned to her home town of Bethlehem. Ruth didn't have any assurance, any guarantee that things would work out. Israelites usually had nothing to do with Moabite people. How would people treat her, a foreigner? Would she be able to find work? What if her bitter mother-in-law became impossible to live with? Would she, Ruth, ever have opportunity to marry again, to have children? All these questions must have filled her mind as the two women trudged those 100 dusty miles to Bethlehem.

But still she went. She went *in spite of* her doubts. After our two babies died, I was still ready to obey God, to go where He called me. But I decided that if I made any requests of Him, I'd end them with "if." "If it glorifies you. If it is your will"—and I'd hope that wasn't showing a lack of faith. Learning to trust God *in spite of* all our unanswered questions is a lifelong discipline.

Choosing faith

We need to begin from childhood to let our theology shape and control our emotions. We can't help those fickle, unpredictable emotions from sweeping over us, sometimes threatening to submerge us. But we *can* control our responses. We need discipline—the kind Paul meant when he wrote about taking captive every thought to make it obedient to Christ (2 Cor. 10:5).

As we think, so we are. As we think, so we become.

But even when we practice it doesn't always work out that neatly. Before cancer invaded my friend Elaine's body, many came to her for help. She gave of herself generously, and her ministry touched many lives. But now as that wretched disease continues its invasion, she has become depressed. "I wish I could die," she says, and sighs deeply. I don't know how to help her. I hold her hand, sit with her, and pray silently. I know she needs to grab hold of hope, to make every day beautiful in spite of the pain and misery. To anticipate life where there will be no more pain and she will be at home with her Lord. But how can I help her latch on to that hope?

Jesus, reach out and touch her.

Faith came singing into my room,
And other guests took flight;
Fear and Anxiety, Grief and Gloom,
Sped out into the night.

I wondered that such peace could be,
But Faith said gently, "Don't you see?
They really cannot live with me."

Author unknown

Nothing We Can Do

D epression and despair are two unpleasant and unwelcome companions who walk alongside us when we are grieving. Sometimes both of them walk with us together, and sometimes just one of them. How do we know which is which? What causes them? And what can we do to be free from them?

In his book *Grief and Growth*, R. Scott Sullender differentiates between the two. He defines "depression" as internalized anger. "Despair, on the other hand, can be defined as hopelessness. Despair is future oriented, whereas depression is past oriented. In despair, the future seems dark, pointless and without meaning. In depression, the past is unfinished, still coloring the present."[1]

Causes of depression

We can expect a certain amount of depression for no particular reason after we have lost a loved one. Even under normal circumstances, when everything is going well, we sometimes feel depressed. Those feelings intensify when we have lost someone dear to us.

---

[1] R. Scott Sullender, *Grief and Growth* (New Jersey: Paulist Press, 1985).

Unexpressed anger, either anger at others or anger at ourselves can cause depression. In addition, anger and low self-esteem (a result of the loss we've experienced) can also produce depression. When I could not carry our babies full term, I felt flawed, lacking, and inadequate. I felt I wasn't any good as a mother.

Many women define their status, respect, social life, and friends through their husbands. When their husbands die, much of their self-esteem and a sense of importance crumbles. And when a husband's death sharply reduces his widow's income, forcing her to move to more modest housing, her sense of self-esteem may suffer further. Depression may result.

Relief for depression

In addition to ascertaining whether or not we are hiding anger that we need to deal with, just giving more attention to our physical needs can help. We need to eat well-balanced meals, drink enough fluids, and get adequate rest and exercise. When we are grieving, we need to give extra attention to caring for our bodies.

Paying attention to grooming also can help. When we are plunged into sorrow, and life loses its savor, we may be tempted to become careless about how we look. Women who stay at home are especially prone to drag around in a bathrobe, neglecting to shower, to brush their hair, or to put on make up. But what we see reflected in the mirror affects how we feel.

Getting out among people and finding new interests helps too. Elisabeth Elliot warns against self-pity. "I know of nothing more paralyzing, more deadly," she writes. "It is a sinkhole from which no rescuing hand can drag you because you have chosen to sink. But it must be refused."

Most often, when depression comes with a loss, it gradually fades as healing takes place. In some cases, if a person has been troubled with depression before, the depression may become severe enough to demand professional help.

Facing despair versus facing depression

Lethargy, apathy, and hopelessness control persons who are despairing. They see no reason to go on living. They feel God has abandoned them. They aren't even sure God exists. Despair is essentially a spiritual problem.

The person who is despairing needs to have hope quickened again. Prayer and worship offer help. So does the support of empathetic friends. Some find it effective when a caring one, in love, challenges them to make statements of faith, even if they must do so without feeling. Repeating and thinking through the Apostle's Creed can be stabilizing. Deliberately thanking God for His love in times past and for His promises to meet our present needs can help too. We can quote the psalmist aloud:

> Though you have made me see troubles, many and bitter, you will restore my life again; from the depths of the earth you will bring me up. You will increase my honor and comfort me once again. I will praise you with the harp for your faithfulness, O my God. I will sing praises to you with the lyre, O Holy One of Israel. My lips will shout for joy when I sing praise to you—I, whom you have redeemed. My tongue will tell of your righteous acts all day long. (Ps. 71:20–24)

Repeating and hearing the promises of God's steadfastness bring stability and encouragement.

Paul Gerhardt, whose hymns we love and sing, bears eloquent testimony to how it is possible to learn to praise God instead of despairing.

The son of the mayor of a town near Wittenberg, Gerhardt entered Wittenberg University when he was 21. But the Thirty Years War interrupted his studies. Not until 14 years later, as a 35-year-old man, was he able to return to Wittenberg to complete his studies. Marriage was delayed for him until he was 48, when he married Anna Marie Barthold, the daughter of a lawyer. But the happiness and comfort of a home filled with laughter, chattering children, and a healthy, hearty wife was denied him. Anna Marie gave birth to five children, but one by one they died. Shortly after their fourth child died, Anna Marie died.

Gerhardt was left to care for a six-year-old son.

The war dragged on, profoundly affecting Gerhardt's writings. His hymns reflect the comfort and consolation he received from a warm, personal relationship with God.

Gerhardt's hymns consistently sounded notes of praise and joy. "Awake, My Heart, with Gladness," and "Soul, Adorn Yourself with Gladness," are only two examples. In "If God Himself Be for Me," Gerhardt declared:

> For joy my heart is ringing;
> All sorrow now disappears;
> And full of mirth and singing,
> It wipes away all tears.[2]

Although Gerhardt emphasized praising God even in the midst of sorrow, he did not minimize, deny, or ignore the pain of bereavement and loss. But when he wrote of death, he always struck a note of triumph. "Of death I am no more afraid," he wrote in "A Lamb Goes Uncomplaining Forth."

Gerhardt's hymns pulsate with a warm, loving devotion to Christ. He addressed the Lord as "my dearest friend," "my joy," "my treasure," "my crown," "my splendor," "my sun," and "my light." Perhaps these terms more than anything else reveal the secret as to why Gerhardt could say, as Paul Tournier, the Swiss doctor, said after his wife died, "I have a great grief, and I am a happy man."[3]

---

[2]Paul Gerhardt, "If God Himself Be for Me," *Lutheran Book of Worship* (Minneapolis, Minn.: Augsburg Publishing House).
[3]Paul Tournier, *Creative Suffering* (San Francisco: Harper & Row Publishers, Inc.).

Let the past sleep,
but let it sleep on the bosom of Christ,
and go out into the irresistible future with Him."

Oswald Chambers[1]

[1]Oswald Chambers, *My Utmost for His Highest* (New York: Dodd, Mead & Co., Publishers, 1935).

I Wish I Had . . .

13

At Mother's funeral I was startled when her former pasor paid tribute to her and referred to her as "Harriet." I was used to "Mother," "Grandma," "Aunt," "Hattie"—which was what her sisters called her—even "Mrs. Hasselquist," as her Sunday-school students addressed her. But "Harriet" set her apart from all roles. Harriet sounded like Mildred. A person.

I began to wonder what Harriet the person had been like. What had been her childhood dreams? What unfulfilled aspirations had lingered on in her heart?

I recalled one unexpected visit a couple of years earlier. When I arrived, I found Mother raking leaves from the maple trees that shaded her front lawn. When she saw me, she leaned her rake against a tree. "I've been thinking it was time for coffee," she said. We dawdled over coffee, but after a few minutes she arose abruptly. Pulling on her worn, heavy, blue garden sweater she said, "Let's go outside." I followed. She headed straight for one of the piles of faded rust and amber leaves she had raked together. Striding right into the middle, she began to kick with the delight of a three-year-old.

"Come on," she called, "it's lots of fun." I stared. She called again. Still I resisted, a fussy, middle-aged woman reluctant to get dusty, while my child-mother sent leaves soaring high into the air. I was dumfounded.

Regrets

After Mother died and I continued to reflect, I realized that from time to time she had given me other brief glimpses of Harriet the person. But I had rushed so hurriedly through life that I had rarely noted them or taken the time to explore further. "You're so busy you don't take time to live," she had often chided me. Now it was too late for me to watch and encourage Harriet the person, though I could still take time to get to know my friends and my immediate family better.

A few years later another regret in regard to my relationship with Mother surfaced. I could no longer easily handle a household of people needing to be bedded and fed. I thought of how old Mother was when our whole family had descended on her for a couple of weeks. *Why wasn't I more thoughtful, more considerate, while she was living?* I thought remorsefully. *Why had I always taken her hospitality for granted?* I discovered the inevitable regret that accompanies bereavement.

Saying "I love you"

If we have enjoyed an intimate relationship with one who has died, we wonder how adequately we met that person's need for love. Perhaps we remember with shame how seldom we told or showed our beloved how much we cared. We wonder how much our dear one missed it or longed for it, even though he or she never demanded it. If our loved one was ill for a long time or was confined to a care home, we wonder if we visited often enough.

Even if we have not had a long relationship with the loved one who has died, we still may feel regrets. When our two premature babies were born, they were taken away from me and put into incubators. When they died a short while later, I asked to see them but was told it would be better if I did not.

But I have always regretted that I did not cradle them in my arms and have a chance to weep over them.

Praying for release

Sometimes our feelings of guilt get mixed up with other emotions. When a person is terminally ill and there seems to be no hope for recovery, when death has been a long time coming, we pray for release. But we may, nevertheless, feel guilty when death finally comes.

Facing unhappy relationships

Endless are the regrets and deep the feelings of guilt when the relationship with the deceased was not a happy one. We realize we are at least partly to blame; we should have been more helpful, more understanding. We wince at the memory of cutting remarks we made. Misunderstandings or differences of opinion erected walls between us. Or maybe our absence from home or our preoccupation with work broke our relationship. Memory after memory surfaces, and with each one feelings of guilt and regret assail us.

Taking responsibility for death

Perhaps the most difficult feeling of guilt to handle occurs when the bereaved feels he or she has been responsible for the death.

A friend of mine experienced this guilt over the death of his son. Just before he and his wife went out one evening, he placed a lamp into a macrame hanging. He left the lamp burning. Their son was sound asleep upstairs when the macrame caught fire, and he did not awaken in time to be saved.

Other parents have agonized over permission they gave their children to go scuba diving, swimming, mountain climbing, or hunting, only to have the outing end in the accidental death of their precious offspring. One mother left medicine within reach of a toddler, and the little one ate it and died. A father left a loaded gun out and his son shot himself.

Whatever the situation, parents feel guilty. "I can't forgive myself," they say. We feel their anguish, but at the same time we need to reassure them that God can do what they can't. God can set them free through confession and forgiveness. If release does not come, these troubled souls should seek professional help; if the load of guilt is not lifted, it can destroy them.

Unjustified guilt

Some of our feelings may not be justified. The freedom from struggling to maintain a harmonious relationship with a touchy, jealous, or cantankerous relative actually can be a relief. We need not feel ashamed or guilty admitting this. Instead, with joy, we can accept our new freedom and move on to a fuller life with God and others.

Dealing With Guilt and Regret

Guilt may be an inevitable part of grieving, but it does not have to control or destroy us. We can take steps to deal with our guilt and free ourselves from its power.

Seek and accept forgiveness

If we *know* we were at fault, we can confess and accept forgiveness. I often pray: "Dear God, I want to confess to you the sins I know I have committed (I then name specific sins that are troubling me). Thank you that Jesus has already suffered for these. Thank you that you are willing to forgive me. I accept your forgiveness. Help me to learn from the wrongs I've committed so I won't do them again."

Chances are our prayers won't sound as calm as this written prayer does, but rather will be accompanied with tears and sighs. Fortunately, when we are through spilling out everything, we can know we are forgiven.

Write letters

Some people find relief not only in confessing to God, but also in writing a letter to the deceased and making confession. Letters provide an outlet for expression and a tangible evidence of our awareness of sin. We can direct our confession to the one we have hurt and find peace in forgiveness.

Learn from mistakes and faults

If we have erred, we can seek to learn from our unintentional actions. Joanette Jorgenson's little daughter Lisa started vomiting on a Tuesday, Joanette's routine cleaning day. Joanette thought she had the flu. By Wednesday Lisa began to scream and pull her hair. Joanette rushed her to the doctor, who rushed her to the hospital. Sunday morning Lisa died, a victim of Reye's Syndrome.

"Tuesday, the day Lisa became ill, I was cleaning the house," Joanette remembered. "I used to take pride in being an immaculate housekeeper and rigidly followed my routine. I snatched only a few minutes to read a book to Lisa that day, the last day she was conscious. I've never been tied to a schedule since. Now *people* get priority over cleaning and schedules."

Accept your loved one's words of reassurance

Robert Hansen of Nebraska noted that part of grief is looking back and wondering if something more might have been done. After his wife, Harriet, died, friends reassured him he had done what he could. His doctor told him the same. "But what helped most of all," he said, "was the night my wife Harriet turned to me and said, 'If I don't make it, I want you to know that I realize you have done what you could.' "[2] When doubts surfaced, Hansen recalled her assurance and received comfort.

---

[2]Robert P. Hansen, from an article published in *The Lutheran Standard* (Minneapolis, Minn.). Permission granted by Robert P. Hansen.

Let go of the past

We need to leave the past with God. In faith, hope, and trust, assured of God's forgiveness and tender understanding, we can turn away from that which has brought us so much anguish. We don't have to carry our regrets and feelings of guilt with us. Instead, like the Apostle Paul, we vow to forget what is behind. We strain (that is, we devote our energy and attention) toward what is ahead as we press on toward the goal to win the prize to which God has called us.

"You've had as much excitement as you should,"
Our mother very often used to say.
"The fun you've had won't do you any good
Till it has settled down in you to stay.
Go listen to the creek and nibble cress,
Go count the grass and catch up to your living."
So we would revel in green idleness
And never realize what she was giving.

A chance to savor new experience slowly
And thoroughly, assimilating all
Its deep significance, till it was wholly
Our own, past any possible recall.
"No use to give them things," she always knew,
"Unless you give them time to keep them, too."

Jane Merchant[1]

[1]Jane Merchant, "Growing Days," from *The Greatest of These Is Love* (Nashville, Tenn.: Abingdon Press). Copyright renewal © 1982 by Elizabeth Merchant. Used by permission of Abingdon Press.

Storytelling

14

*T*his is the room where Mother died," the nursing supervisor told me. Not "your Mother," but "Mother," I noted. It reflected the close relationship the staff sought to have with their patients. The funeral was over, and I had come to thank the extended care unit for their loving care of Mother during her last days.

The room was empty now, but I stood there for a few minutes, the nursing supervisor waiting silently by my side. As I turned to go, she said, "Why don't we go to my private office and visit for a few minutes?"

She reconstructed for me in careful detail Mother's last days and nights. As she did so, I was able to visualize the scenes. She told me everything, even those things that were painful to hear. With tears I thanked her.

After I returned home, I wrote letters to our children scattered in many cities and related the story of Grandma's death. When I spoke with dear friends who would take the time to listen, I also found myself telling them just how it had been. And as I talked, I began to understand what had happened many years earlier.

My father died when I was 20. Shortly after Father died, Mother had to undergo surgery. She went into a coma, and we kept anxious vigil for a number of days. When she finally came out of her coma, pneumonia attacked her. For weeks she lay in bed at home. I quit my job to go home and care for her and the family, and stayed on for a number of months. Those months, as Mother was working through her grief, she related over and over to me the last weeks and days that father had lived. I wondered if the storytelling would ever cease. Now, years later, as I felt a compulsion to tell others how Mother had died, I began to understand how telling the story over and over helps us come to terms with the reality of the death and eventually makes it easier to bear.

Storytelling as ritual

Telling our story need not be limited to verbalization. When we left East Africa and returned to the States to live, David, who had been born on Kilimanjaro, was just seven years old. Leaving Africa for him meant leaving home, playmates, pet cat, and all that was dear and familiar to him.

Our African friends had made a tape recording of our farewell service. After we were settled in our U.S. home, David developed a routine. Every day when he came home from school, he would go downstairs to the playroom, play Tanzania's national anthem, and stand at attention. Then he would slip in the tape of our farewell service. Part of the service was a greeting from the principal of the school where my husband had taught. David would play the greeting over and over, then he would come upstairs.

"Did you hear that, Ma?" he would ask. "Pastor Masawe says they'll never forget the Tengbom family."

Day after day he repeated this little ritual. Then one day a playmate came over, and David did not listen to the tape. After that, little by little, the gaps between his playings of the tape widened. Finally, the trips to the playroom were replaced by a rush outside to play ball with his new friends.

For David, "telling his story" took the form of listening to the voices of loved ones who assured him of their love for him.

102

For the bereaved, storytelling may mean revisiting again and again the site of the death or going to the cemetery frequently. The effect will be the same. The storytelling eases the pain and enables the grieving one to accept the loss and move on.

Getting the facts straight

Before we begin our storytelling, however, we must be careful to get the facts straight so that we stay in touch with reality. This is particularly important if the death was accidental or occurred at a distance from us. What does the police report say? Who witnessed the death? What do the hospital records tell us?

The widow of an abusive alcoholic made an absolute saint of him when she told her story about him. Gently and lovingly, friends had to help her to accept him as the person he had been. We must always stay in touch with reality.

Easing the pain

Storytelling makes the pain more endurable. Like the comfort that callouses offer us compared to the discomfort of blisters, telling the story of a loved one's death accustoms us to the reality of death and enables us to bear it.

Enlarging our understanding

In the novel *Godric*, the main character initially remembers his deceased father as a workaholic, caring little for his children. "Endless was the work. . . . he was ever striding off in every way but ours. . . . A gray gust of a man . . . but wind has no power to comfort a child or lend a strong arm to a lad whose bones are weak with growing. . . . He sits by the hearth, his back as ever turned. . . . He loved us sure, but like the bread a beggar dreams about, his love could never pad the ribs or make the heart grow strong."[2]

---

[2]Frederick Buechner, *Godric* (San Francisco: Harper & Row, Publishers, Inc.). Used by permission of Harper & Row.

Later, in retrospect, Godric pleads with his father, now dead, for forgiveness. "I've chided you for failing as a father, too spent from grubbing to have any love to spend on me," Godric confesses. "Maybe it was the other way around, and it was I that failed you as a son. Did I ever bring you broth? Was any word I ever spoke a word to cheer your weariness?"[3]

Thus Godric not only arrived at a new understanding of his father by telling his story, but also learned how he had failed in *his* relationship to his father.

Identifying our feelings

Even as Godric realized how he had misunderstood and failed his father, he also found himself having to deal with destructive feelings he had cherished toward his father: anger, hostility, even hatred, and finally guilt because of all these negative emotions and attitudes.

Relieving anxiety

As we tell our story we may find ourselves voicing fears and problems that haunt us as we face the future. But as we talk about them, often we gain understanding and see our way through.

Reaffirming hope in the resurrection

On the Sunday after the Resurrection, two of the disciples were walking to Emmaus, about seven miles from Jerusalem. When Jesus came alongside and asked what they had been discussing, they told Him how the crucifixion had crushed their hopes. Hurt and betrayed, they felt foolish because they had allowed themselves to be led on.

Jesus encouraged them to continue, and they told Him about the women's visit to the empty tomb. Jesus began to explain to them what the Scriptures taught about all this. Hope flickered

---

[3]Ibid.

in their hearts. Was it possible that these events made some sense after all?

Jesus came in with them, and as they ate their meal, suddenly they recognized Him, and He disappeared. "Didn't our hearts burn when He spoke with us?" they asked each other. They recognized the illumination His Word brings and its mysterious power.

Hurrying back to Jerusalem they told their friends, "It's true! The Lord has risen!" As the disciples told their story and voiced their doubts and questions, Jesus was able to quicken hope in their hearts by pointing them to the hope of resurrection.

We can also feel free to tell our story. And when others tell theirs, we can listen and help each other to see the truth of the resurrection.

Finding understanding listeners

Finding a listener who won't be shocked, who won't interrupt, and who won't contradict us by telling us we didn't fail or injure the deceased when we *know* we did, can help immensely in dealing with sin that we recognize as we tell our stories. We need a listener who will allow and encourage us to make confession and then pronounce to us God's word of forgiveness.

If we doubt we can find a human friend we can trust in this way, we can always turn to our loving, compassionate, merciful, and understanding heavenly Father. We can tell things to Him just as they are. He knows we're not perfect. No one cares for us or understands as He does.

Nurture strength of spirit
to shield you in sudden misfortune.
But do not distress yourself with imaginings.
Many fears are born of fatigue and loneliness,
Beyond a wholesome discipline,
Be gentle with yourself.

Desiderata

No coward soul is mine,
No trembler in the world's storm-troubled sphere,
I see Heaven's glories shine
And faith shines equal, arming me from fear.

Emily Bronte

Facing Death

A year ago my sister died. She put up a courageous fight
against cancer for a year, but by January it became clear
that she was going to lose the battle. My brothers and their
wives, who lived close to her, had lovingly cared for her through
a year of hospital stays and time in extended care units as well
as endless trips for treatments.

When I received word that her time was running out, I found
myself pulled many directions. I longed to be with her, to *do*
something for her. At the same time, I didn't want to believe
she was dying, and it was easier to deny it when I was 2,000
miles away. I had just accompanied some friends through painful experiences, and I didn't want to hurt again. "Lord," I cried,
"I've had enough! Do I have to see another grave opened? Another home emptied? Our own family circle shrinking?"

Luverne urged me to go to see her. I stalled, made excuses.
Then one morning I read these words of George MacDonald:

> You can begin at once to be a disciple of the Living One
> by obeying him in the first thing you can think of in which
> you are not obeying him. . . . Let it be at once, and in the
> very next thing that lies at the door of your conscience.[1]

---

[1]George MacDonald, *Creation in Christ* (Wheaton, Ill.: Harold Shaw Publishers,
1976). Copyright Harold Shaw Publishers and used by permission.

As I faced the reason for my procrastination—my unwillingness to be hurt again—I was struck silent. I got up and began to phone for information about flight schedules.

Although the decision brought peace, unspoken anxieties continued to live in my mind. I had no questions about Alma's relationship with God. She had maintained a quiet, unassuming, faithful walk with Him all her life. But I wondered how death would come for her.

That question was foremost in my mind on Alma's last night as it became more and more apparent to me that she was, indeed, dying. Would she lose consciousness? Secretly I wished she would; somehow I felt it would be easier for *me* if she slipped into a coma first. But the nurse could not assure me this would happen. Instead, she said to me, "Your sister might be conscious to the end."

Her words increased my fear. I had heard from friends of the death struggles of their loved ones that had been heart-wrenching to watch.

In Alma's case, death came peacefully. As the long hours of the night passed slowly, I grew weary as I sat by her bedside. I was not aware of how Alma's labored breathing was exhausting her completely.

Around two A.M. a nurse came in and pushed the empty bed in the room up to Alma's bed. "Lie down," she ordered. "I've brought a blanket for you." Then, going over to Alma's bed, she and the attendant gently turned Alma's frail body so she could lie facing me. We lay there, two sisters, facing each other, holding hands, awaiting death quietly, calmly, almost in a matter-of-fact way approaching that stupendous mystery that forever baffles us.

Alma was restless, but not agitated. "Pain?" I would question. She would shake her head. "Tired?" She would nod but then smile. Her tracheotomy wouldn't allow her to talk.

As time passed I could trace the relentless progress of oncoming death as its chill moved from fingers to wrist to lower arm, to elbow, and upwards from her feet to her legs. Once when the nurse came to check on her, I slipped out to go to the rest room. When I came back, Alma was restlessly turning her head from side to side. "She's looking for you," the nurse said. I lay down and took her hand, and instantly she was quiet.

At five A.M something told me the end was very near. I got up. "You're cold," I said. I tucked my blanket around her.

"It's five A.M., February 1," I said. "Alison's (my grandchild and her grandniece) second birthday."

A smile of joy brightened her face and unexpectedly set my tears flowing. Cradling her in my arms, I told her again how much we all loved her. Her breathing was very shallow. The whistling through the opening in her throat had stopped. Her blue eyes, enormous now, remained focused on me, comprehending, loving. I bathed her with my tears, feeling the exquisite agony and pain of those last moments: my utter helplessness, my irrational desire to hang on to the life that was slipping away from me, the near panic gripping me causing me to ring again and again for the nurse as though she could come and miraculously prevent life from ebbing away. Hope persists beyond human reason. And then all was very, very quiet.

There are many kinds of silences, and each means a different thing. In silence, all the leaves on the trees hang motionless just before a tornado tears across the land. Immediately after an earthquake, silence descends when the earth has ceased swaying and creaking. After an aged spouse has died, or after the last child has moved away, silence invades the home. After someone has made an embarrassing remark, an awkward silence comes. And a profound silence reigns when a person stops breathing.

I dialed my brother's number but had difficulty talking. Then I called a friend, Thyra, to come and pick me up. I gathered together Alma's belongings and stood alone at her bedside. Finally I untied from her bed the silver "We love you" balloon our daughter Janet had brought her a few days earlier. A nurse walked with me to the lobby to wait for Thyra.

It was still dark when we stepped outside. Stars studded the deep black sky. Freshly fallen snow crunched under our feet. I put the silver balloon in the back of the car, but before I could close the door, it escaped. Thyra and I stood watching it sail higher and higher, another star, it seemed, headed for another home. And then we hugged each other, our tears mingling.

Why, I wondered later, *was I so totally human those last hours?* I had dreaded death, dreaded it because it would once again remind me of my own mortality, dreaded it because I didn't want to be hurt. I was afraid because I didn't know what form death would take; if it was prolonged, agonized, and tormented, I didn't know if I would have the courage to face it.

When it became apparent that most of the hours were going to be peaceful, I felt no urge to repeat Bible verses to Alma. It had seemed unnecessary to me. Both of us felt we were "resting in the everlasting arms," that we were being carried. Two stanzas of a children's hymn that I had not thought of for years echoed and re-echoed in my mind that night.

> Jesus, tender shepherd, hear me,
> Bless thy little lamb tonight.
> Through the darkness be thou near me,
> Keep me safe till morning light.

> May my sins be all forgiven
> Bless the friends I love so well,
> Take me, Lord, at last to heaven,
> Happy there with thee to dwell.

What will it be like when my time comes to die? I have no way, no way at all, of knowing. G. H. Knight, in his book *In the Cloudy and Dark Day,* noted:

> There is a light sometimes upon a dying face that reflects a hidden sun, and murmurs are heard on dying lips that seem snatches of the songs of heaven. But it is not always so; indeed it is rarely so. Such glowing transports in the dying hour are quite exceptional. They cannot be calculated upon; and the want of them need throw no doubt upon the reality of Christian faith.
>
> Very few Christians die in ecstasy. Every true Christian is a conqueror over death and absolutely safe; but not every one has a song of victory on the dying lips. Only a few Elijahs here and there go home in a chariot of fire. The largest part

of God's redeemed host are carried out of sight in a chariot of cloud. In weakness of body and weariness of mind hardly a word is uttered, and all around the bed are falling tears.

Some, indeed, have even less than this. They die amid the shadows, trembling lest they should be castaways. Still, God's redeemed and loved are just as safe in the chariot of cloud as in the chariot of fire. The victory is real, though the song of victory is reserved for the other side.[2]

Knight's words are particularly comforting, for sometimes I have wondered what it will be like after I cross that dividing ridge into the unknown of eternity. At times, as I have thought of actually appearing before the unfathomable, mysterious God—the Other One, the One set apart from all of us, totally holy, totally righteous—I have trembled. In fact, I have not had the courage to let myself think about it too long. I know, to some degree—God knows me better than I know myself—how far short I have fallen. Though the sacrifice of His Son absolves me and justifies me in His sight, still He calls me to strive to live a righteous life. And my striving too often has been half-hearted, my commitment flawed with too many reservations and excuses, and my love for Him and others made subservient to my own self-love.

Maybe it is wise not to dwell on this fear too much, beyond letting it be a call to me for a closer walk with God. For in the end, no matter how anxious my fears, no matter how deeply doubts may disturb me, in the end God's covenant made with me remains firm and irrevocable. God will not go back on His promises to me. The sacrifice of His Son is all I have to cling to, but it is enough.

Although God the Father, God the Creator, God the Judge, and God the Holy Spirit seem beyond my human comprehension, this same God chose to reveal himself in His Son. When I live in fellowship with Him, listen to Him and especially when I hear Him praying for me, I know that whatever comes, He

[2]G. H. Knight, *In the Cloudy and Dark Day* (Rock Island, Ill.: Augustana Book Concern, 1934).

will see me through. George MacDonald's prayer has become the prayer of my heart:

Yester eve Death came and knocked at my door,
I from my window looked. The thing I saw,
the shape uncouth, I had not seen before.
I was disturbed—with fear, in sooth, not awe.
Wherefore, ashamed, I instantly did rouse
My will to see Thee—only to fear the more.
Alas! I could not find Thee in the house.

I was like Peter when he began to sink.
To Thee a new prayer therefore I have got—
that, when Death comes in earnest to my door,
Thou wouldst Thyself go, when latch doth clink,
And lead him to my room, up to my cot,
Then hold Thy child's hand, hold and leave him not,
Till Death has done with him forevermore.

Till Death has done with him? Ah, leave me then?
And Death has done with me, oh, nevermore!
He comes and goes to leave me in Thy arms,
Nearer Thy heart, oh, nearer than before!
To lay Thy child, naked, new born again
Of mother-earth, crept free through many harms,
Upon Thy bosom—still to the very core.

But we have this treasure in jars of clay to show that this all-surpassing power is from God and not from us. We are hard pressed on every side, but not crushed; perplexed, but not in despair; persecuted, but not abandoned; struck down, but not destroyed. . . . It is written: "I believed; therefore I have spoken." With that same spirit of faith we also believe and therefore speak, because we know that the one who raised the Lord Jesus from the dead will also raise us with Jesus and present us with you in his presence. Therefore we do not lose heart. Though outwardly we are wasting away, yet inwardly we are being renewed day by day. . . . So we fix our eyes not on what is seen, but on what is unseen. For what is seen is temporary, but what is unseen is eternal. . . . Now we know that if the earthly tent we live in is destroyed, we have a building from God, an eternal house in heaven, not built by human

hands. . . . Therefore we are always confident and know that as long as we are at home in the body we are away from the Lord. We live by faith, not by sight.
    2 Cor. 4:7–9, 14, 16, 18; 5:1, 6, 7

Much of what we call evil
is due entirely to the way people take the
*   phenomenon.*
It can so often be converted
into a bracing and tonic good
by a simple change of the sufferer's inner attitude
from one of fear to one of fight.

William James

After Death

Because Mother and I were both older, and because I long before had established a life independent from her, I did not experience many of the anxieties and fears that may follow the loss of a younger loved one. But those anxieties are very real for many bereaved, and they must be faced.

Anxiety about the future

People often wonder how they will manage to face the future without their loved one. They feel like crying out with Job, "What strength do I have, that I should still hope?" (Job 6:8).

We wonder if we can carry on by ourselves. We fear the unknown, and cannot imagine that life will go on. Yet we amaze ourselves as we discover abilities, strength, and determination we had never tapped before.

One woman, before her husband died, always complained of frail health. Her husband did practically everything for her. But after he died, she surprised everybody with her energy. She lived 20 years more, and at age 80 was still mowing her own lawn.

Fear of putting feelings into words

"I couldn't admit my anger at God," another widow confessed. "I was afraid He'd punish me if I told Him." But her image of God was distorted and needed gentle correction, for God is able to deal with our anger and grief.

Fear because of eerie experiences

"A few nights after my husband died, I awakened, sure that my husband was in bed with me," a young widow said. Another reported, "I was preparing dinner at night when, I swear, I heard the door open and my husband come in." Experiences like this shake us up. We wish we could talk to someone, but we don't dare.

But these eerie experiences need not alarm us. They're quite normal. At a time of grief, our whole system is upset. Our perception is distorted. Our brain may send us messages that are geared more to what we want to experience than to what is real. A widow may long to feel her husband's body in bed with her. She may yearn to have him walk in the door. Our desires can become so powerful that our brain interprets any sound as the familiar, welcome one we used to hear.

When we experience some of these strange things, we needn't worry. We're not going crazy. Many, perhaps most, grieving people have similar experiences. But the incidents won't go on forever.

Bringing our fears to God

Disclosing our fears to a close friend, as well as talking to God about them, can help. Try to imagine what God would say in response. Are our fears groundless, or so great that He cannot give us courage to face them? What are our alternatives as we face problems? What avenues of help are available for us? Who can help us? As we set aside time every day to sit in God's presence, seeking His guidance and direction, we shall be astonished to experience how God does indeed guide.

Paul Tournier, a Swiss physician, in his book *Fatigue in Modern Society*, tells of a friend who came to him at the beginning of the war in 1939. "Arnold Mugle," Tournier writes, "was one of those puny men who always appear to be at the end of their strength, often ill, and to whom physicians are compelled to recommend that they live very restricted lives." The Swiss federal government had commissioned Mugle to take charge of food rationing. Faced with the prospect of being surrounded by the German armies and their allies, the Swiss people's only hope of survival lay in careful planning. Mugle wondered how he could carry this heavy load of responsibility. Tournier suggested they commit the matter to God and together wait in silence before God for his guidance. According to Tournier:

> My friend, afterward, read to me what he had written in his notebook during that moment of silence. "I will not live at Berne; I will leave my family at Zurich; I will go to Berne from Monday morning to Friday evening, in order to be able to give myself to my work without being split between it and my family. . . . (One cause of fatigue is a division between several duties which impedes concentration.) On Friday evening I will return home to Zurich in order to devote all of Saturday to reflecting tranquilly on the major problems which one never has the time to think about when one is pestered by the telephone in the office. . . . (Another frequent cause of fatigue is the lack of time to reflect on essentials because one is taken up with incidentals.) Finally, on Sunday, I will cease to work, and I will give myself entirely to my family." This is what he did, and he assumed his task with so much authority and wisdom that the University of Zurich named him Doctor of Medicine *Honoris causa*. And at the end of the war he was in infinitely better health than before.[1]

Tournier goes on to point out the value of organizational measures as well as knowing on whom to unload certain of our tasks instead of assuming all of them ourselves. Wisdom for

---

[1]Paul Tournier, *Fatigue in Modern Society* (Richmond, Va.: John Knox Press, 1965). © Labor Et Fides S.A., Genéve, Switzerland. Used by permission.

understanding how to do this can come from our quiet times when we wait for instruction from God.

Many individuals are also able to draw courage from reading the Psalms; often they are a kind of running dialogue with God. Innumerable examples of people who found courage to meet their fears are found in the Bible, and reading these accounts can bolster our courage as well.

We need to remember that Christ is no stranger to what we are experiencing. "We do not have a high priest who is unable to sympathize with our weaknesses," the writer of Hebrews declared, "but we have one who has been tempted in every way just as we are, yet was without sin. Let us then approach the throne of grace with confidence, so that we may receive mercy and find grace to help us in our time of need " (Heb. 4:15–16).

The off-key wind is whistling through its teeth
While strings are tuned by pizzicato rain;
The bare bough scrapes against my lonesome
room,
Rapping its knuckles on my windowpane.

My winter's hearth is losing summer's glow,
I'll make some coffee, pour a cup of cheer,
Play records ... read a book—it is no use,
The fingering chill comes on ... and you not here.

Ralph W. Seager[1]

---

[1]Ralph W. Seager, "Lonely Hearth" from *Wheatfields and Vineyards* (New York: Christian Herald House, 1975). Copyright held by Ralph W. Seager and used by permission.

The Pain of Separation

M onths after Mother died I noted in my journal:

At Good Friday services this year I experienced
what I've heard people talk about before, how listening to talk
about death and dying can be almost unbearably painful. Pastor Greg was talking about dying, and the last days I was with
Mother came back to me so vividly that my jaws and teeth
began to ache!

A few weeks ago a friend, whose young adult son had just
been killed in an accident, asked, "Why does bereavement hurt
so much? I never have known such awful, awful pain, right
here." He thumped his chest. "Will I ever feel normal and whole
again?"

Grief does hurt. Otto Rank, Harry Stack Sullivan, and David Switzer, all of whom have written extensively about bereavement, define grief as separation anxiety, or the fear that
grips us because we are losing part of our very selves when a
loved one dies.

Early separation

While the fear of separation through death may be more
profoundly disturbing than any other, still the pain of separation

is no stranger to us. Psychologists tell us we first experience this pain of separation when we are born. A baby gets used to his mother's voice while he is still cradled within her. Mother represents security, and when birth separates the baby from his mother's body, the fear of further separation lingers. *Learned* trust and attachments to parents, siblings, friends, and spouse replace that fear. Trust alleviates anxiety and gives us the courage to find a separate existence.

Inevitable separation

We grow up, leave home, and go away to school or work. Maybe we don't feel the pangs of separation too keenly because of our strong, youthful urge for independence. But our parents feel it!

We make another break if we get married. Caught up in a new love relationship, the pain of separation from parents is dulled for the newlyweds. But their parents feel it, and they spill tears at the wedding.

These separations bring pain not only because we are saying goodbye to a relationship we have previously enjoyed but because hidden in these events are reminders that time has moved on, and down the road we sense the ultimate parting from loved ones that death brings.

Avoiding the issue

But who wants to think about death? So we push aside the thought. At weddings we blot our tears, laugh, kiss the bride and groom, and hurry off to the reception hall to greet the guests. And when the celebration is over, we resolutely push down the sadness and plunge into work again.

Unfortunately, in doing so we pass by an opportunity to prepare ourselves, at least in some small measure, for the separation that death will bring. And because we avoid facing the intermediate separations of life, the day death takes away one of our loved ones, we are unprepared to deal with the pain of separation.

Separation brings loneliness

The loneliness from loss of a loved one might be easier to face if our friends didn't absent themselves also. They are available during the first days following the death. But after a while, as Martin Marty expressed in *A Cry of Absence*, "They have their own coffee pots to put on, their own paychecks to draw, their own bright moments to celebrate."[2]

Jesus understands our pain

When others forsake us, we can turn to Jesus, who understands in a way that no one else can. He experienced to a singular degree the pain of separation, the chilling fear, and the distressing anxiety that accompany it.

For Jesus, the human One, knew the pain of separation from loved ones the night before He was to die. Those closest to Him, whom He had asked to watch with Him, slept. Worn out with sorrow (Luke 22:45), they could not support Jesus when He needed it most. Later, when Jesus was captured and death grew more imminent, "all the disciples deserted him and fled" (Matt. 26:56). Jesus looked around. No one was left.

Later Peter came creeping back, hoping not to be recognized. When he was identified, fear mastered him. "I'm not one of His!" he declared. Even when guilt overcame Peter and he repented, he still left Jesus alone, alone to bear the separation caused by Peter's sin . . . and yours and mine.

And because Jesus picked up and bore our sins, He faced a far more painful separation than we ever will. "I and the Father are one," He had attested. But the consequence of sin is separation from God, and in bearing our sin, Jesus had to experience that separation. His physical death on the cross reflected the

---

[2]Martin Marty, *A Cry of Absence* (San Francisco: Harper and Row Publishers Inc.).

more terrible death that took place. In His death He was to be severed from the one with whom He was one. Can such pain be understood? God forsaken by God.

The Old Testament story of Abraham and his son, Isaac, gives us a dim foreshadowing of the supreme agony of the Father in stepping aside and letting His Son die. As they approached the mount where Abraham knew he was supposed to kill his son, Abraham told his servants to stay behind, and "the two of them [father and son] went on together" (Gen. 2:8).

So too, God the Father and God the Son walked together up the hill, neither one drawing back, to the place where a cross would be raised. There the Father stepped aside and let His Son be killed.

When we feel that no one understands how much we hurt—and no one can—we need to remember the anguished cry of Him who struggled to accept the cross which set us free from the fear of death and the fear of ultimate separation from God. "My soul is overwhelmed with sorrow to the point of death" (Matt. 26:38), He cried, even before He got to the hill. And at Golgotha, during His last moments, He called out, "My God, my God, *why have you forsaken me?*" (Matt. 27:46). The one from whom that tortured cry was wrung understands our pain. He understands our sense of aloneness in our sorrow.

So what can we do with the awful tearing pain of separation that comes with bereavement? We can do little except bear it. Unfortunately it is part of the fabric, the work of grief. But those who have suffered through it will tell us that little by little the sharpest pain will diminish. Some of the pain will always be with us, for once we have experienced the loss of a loved one, we are never the same again. But as we trust God, we become better persons.

In mourning, we who are Christians differ from those who do not know Christ. We ache because of the physical separation from our loved one. Yet we differ from Freud, who stressed the necessity of detachment to the point that one of his followers expressed it as "killing the dead person." As Christians, we believe in the communion of saints. We remain attached—perhaps even more closely—to our deceased loved ones. It is an attachment that does not imprison or cripple us, but rather a bond that nourishes us and enables us to grow.

> *Lord, thee I love with all my heart;*
> > *I pray thee, ne'er from me depart;*
> *With tender mercy cheer me.*
> > *Earth has no pleasure I would share,*
> *Yea, heav'n itself were void and bare*
> > *If thou, Lord, wert not near me.*
> *And should my heart for sorrow break,*
> > *My trust in thee can nothing shake.*
> *Thou art the portion I have sought;*
> > *Thy precious blood my soul has bought.*
> *Lord Jesus Christ, My God and Lord, my God and Lord,*
> > *Forsake me not! I trust thy Word.*
>
> *Martin Schalling*[3]

---

[3]Translated by Catherine Winkworth.

What *we meet with in our life*
    is not so terribly important;
the only *important thing*
    is whether we accept it
    as coming from God's hand
    and whether we dare to trust
    that it was made to measure—
    your measure and mine—
    and therefore is exactly right.

Helmut Thielicke[1]

---

[1]Helmut Thielicke, *How the World Began* (Philadelphia, Pa.: Fortress Press). Copyright held by Fortress Press and used by permission.

Acceptance

18

*B*elieving that our loved one has really died and no longer denying it is one thing. Accepting the death—that is, saying, "I don't like it; it causes me awful pain, but I will trust God through it all," is something else. Madame Guyon wrote, "Ah, if you knew what peace there is in an accepted sorrow!"

Acceptance vs. submission or resignation

Margaret Clarkson, in *Grace Grows Best in Winter*, defines submission as giving in *against one's will*, a saying "yes" even when one is still rebelling. One feels there is no choice, and so one submits. Resignation, she believes, can be even more negative and more passive, carrying the seeds of self-pity and self-imposed martyrdom. On the other hand, Clarkson states, acceptance is "taking from God's hand absolutely anything He chooses to give us, looking up into His face in love and trust, even in thanksgiving."[2]

---

[2]Margaret Clarkson, *Grace Grows Best in Winter* (Grand Rapids, Mich.: Wm. B. Eerdmans Publishing Company, 1984).

Difficult acceptance

I vacillated in accepting the reality of Mother's death for months, perhaps because living at a distance made it difficult to realize it had really happened. But to say that it was all right that Mother had died was not too difficult for me. Mother was 85. She had lived a full, meaningful life. And she would not have wanted to continue to live as an invalid.

Accepting the death of our two sons, however, had been extremely difficult. Their deaths caused me to question the love of God and the validity of prayer. I needed to be reassured. Paul Tournier, the Swiss physician, pointed out that in order to accept bereavement of a loved one, one must be assured of God's love. "For me," Tournier wrote, "it is the intimacy with Jesus which commits me to active acceptance, because it is in suffering that I especially perceive His nearness, His presence, His participation in my life. I believe we can face everything when we believe we are loved."[3] George MacDonald repeated this theme in one of his poems:

> Thou workest perfectly. And if it seems
> Some things are not so well, 'tis but because
> They are too loving-deep, too lofty-wise,
> For me, poor child, to understand their laws;
> My highest wisdom half is but a dream;
> My love runs helpless like a falling stream;
> Thy good embraces ill, and lo, its illness dies!

The will to accept

Sometimes acceptance just seems to "happen"; over a period of time we are reassured of God's love. At other times we must *will* to accept, even though we still *feel* rebellious and angry, or we cannot understand how God can be love and still let happen what has happened. Kierkegaard referred to this. He said that from a rational point of view he could only describe God as

---

[3]Paul Tournier, *Creative Suffering* (San Francisco: Harper & Row Publishers Inc.).

cruel, intent on making people unhappy. But, he added, even as this was the only conclusion he could make *rationally*, still he would declare his intention (his will) to assert and believe that God is a God of love and does all out of love.[4] Actually, when bad things happen to us, they test our faith in God's character. We come through that testing when we determine to remain true to what the Bible teaches us about God's character, even if what we see happening appears to contradict the Bible's teachings. In other words, we make a statement of *faith*.

God enables us

We may discover, however, that we cannot make this statement of faith by ourselves. We need God's help. James 1:2–4 says: "Consider it pure joy, my brothers, whenever you face trials of many kinds, because you know that the testing of your faith develops perseverance. Perseverance must finish its work so that you may be mature and complete, not lacking anything." Of course, we humans don't consider facing trials a "pure joy." Therefore, James goes on to say, "If any of you lacks wisdom, he should ask God, who gives generously to all without finding fault, and it will be given to him" (James 1:5).

The New American Standard Version notes that another translation for wisdom could be "an understanding heart," or a "listening heart." In other words, when trials and testings come, and we cannot respond with joy, with an understanding heart, a heart that listens for what God has to say, James says we should ask and God will give it to us.

Later in his letter (3:17) James elaborates on the characteristics of this wisdom or this listening heart: it is pure (single-minded in our desire to glorify God); peace-loving (no longer rebellious); considerate (not demanding); submissive (letting God be God); sincere (true in what we pray for). As God builds in us this kind of a listening heart, acceptance of our loss will become possible.

---

[4]Soren Kierkegaard, *The Last Years* (New York: Harper & Row Publishers Inc., 1965).

After the death of their three-year-old son, Leonore Lowry admitted wondering if ever in her life again she would be able to see a beautiful sunset or hear beautiful music without pain. "I can remember finally saying to God, 'All right. I am not happy, and whether I am happy again is not of great consequence. I will leave that up to you. In whatever time I have left on this earth, let me be useful.'"

Ten years later she wrote: "I am happy. You may find this hard to believe or understand, but I can thank God, without reservation, that we had Stephen, and that he has preceded us to our heavenly home."

Acceptance slowly became possible for me, too. Some of the hurt still remains, especially as I look at our four vibrant adult children and wonder what our other two sons would have been like. But I am also at peace knowing they are safe with our Lord. I am deeply thankful for the family God has given us and for a rich life; looking back at it from today's viewpoint, I would love another chance to live life again.

So as we turn to God for help and receive it, we shall find ourselves able to accept loss. We let the yoke of suffering slip over our shoulders and rest there, assured it was made just for us. We enroll in this new class of pain. Accept the discipline of sorrow. Learn little by little to rise with praise and worship on your lips in the sacrament of pain. As we do so, peace and rest will come. The color will return to the flowers, the melody to the song of the birds, the flavor to food, and a smile to our faces. And we will find ourselves actually wanting to reach out to others in love and compassion.

The winter after he died
She ordered far more
Brilliant seed catalogs
Than ever before.

She had no garden then;
The farm had gone
When he did. The catalogs
Were for hoping on.

Turning the pages of pictures
Of huge, indomitable flowers
She could believe in spring
Through dark frozen hours.

Their children would find a way,
Understanding her basic need
For putting down roots again.
They were grown of good seed.

She had a house and garden
The summer after he died,
And a bundle of seed catalogs
Verified.

Jane Merchant[1]

---

[1]Jane Merchant, "The Winter after He Died," from *Blessed Are You* (Nashville, Tenn.: Abingdon Press). Copyright © 1961 held by Abingdon Press and used by permission.

Finding Meaning in Life Again

19

*E*specially in the gray beginning of our sorrow, when a loved one dies, life loses some of the meaning it once held for us. If our relationship with our deceased one was good, our loved one helped us become who we are. Our beloved affirmed, encouraged and challenged us, as well as eased us through the rough spots in life. Our loved one gave us someone to live for, to work for. Our shared sorrows were lessened; our shared joys multiplied. Life was richer, more buoyant and stimulating when we were loved and gave love. "Music I heard was more than music," Conrad Aiken wrote, "and bread I broke with you was more than bread." So, without question, when we lose a loved one, life loses some of the meaning it once held for us.

Depending on what our relationship was to the one who has died, we may experience other losses, too. If a husband or wife dies, the surviving spouse may lose friends, status, financial security or position, ability to travel, home—the possibilities of loss are many. With each loss, meaning is drained from life.

Life does not, of course, lose all meaning. If we are left with others who love us and whom we love, if we have work we enjoy, if we are in a living relationship with God, then life still holds much meaning for us. When my father died, I lost a parent

133

who loved and understood me. But I had already made the break from home. I was planning on working overseas. I enjoyed close and intimate relationships with friends. Life still held much meaning for me.

For those whose lives have been closely intertwined with and dependent on the deceased loved one, the first waves of grief may be overwhelming. All they can think about is how they loved and were loved, and how everything has changed now.

But life must go on. As time passes and sorrow's cutting edges dull, we will again feel the need to rediscover meaning for life—and seek ways to do so.

Discovering

As we seek to pick up and go on, allowing time and God's grace to heal our brokenness, we can discover new ways in which He wants to work. Every transition involves loss of some kind, and in every transitional phase of life, growth occurs only as we search for it. We need an inquiring mind that asks, "God, what do you have in this for me?"

After asking and listening, we need to seek and explore. We can find new friendships, deepen relationships with existing loved ones, discover ways to fill hours of loneliness. We can develop skills that will enable us to carry on, and reach out to others who need help.

"For many years I had dreamed of returning to school," Vivian Johnson said. "When Todd [her 15-year-old son] died, I realized that life is short and decided to get on with my goal. I also realized no one would take me by the hand and bring me to the university. I had to do it myself. Returning from the university that registration day, I caught myself humming, something I hadn't done for several months. I had a goal."

Meaning in work

If we previously gave too much time, energy and attention to our work, we may need to cut back. Or, as we review the

134

meaningfulness of our loved one's work, we may be challenged and inspired to do our work more diligently.

After his wife Harriet died, Robert Hansen wrote, in an article in *The Lutheran Standard*, what she would have wanted:

> For instance, there are four children whom she loved; obviously she would want them raised in the best possible way. She was devoted to her Lord and the church, so that means that work is still tremendously important and must go on. I also must remind myself that she loved life and her time of fun, and so we must have portions of that also. C. S. Lewis said he discovered, 'the less I mourn her, the nearer I seem to her.' "[2]

If a loved one died with an unfulfilled dream, we may feel called to fulfill it. This was true for an acquaintance of mine named Charles. When his older brother who was studying for the ministry died, Charles sensed a call from God to the ministry. Many fruitful, joyful years followed.

Meaning in richer relationships

Death, or the threat of it, is the best values clarification process God has yet devised. Suddenly we are forced to stop and think. What is most important to us—loving relationships, antiques, grand houses, advancements, financial success, status, recognition?

During the Vietnam War, in the days of the Saigon evacuation, many were fleeing in haste. At the airfield, one mother pushed her children along ahead of her while she herself staggered under what evidently was a very heavy suitcase. Once on the plane, she dropped her case and told two of her children to watch it while she ran back to pick up the youngest, a toddler who had fallen behind, and carry him on board. But just as she was about to exit, she saw the door close, and she felt the plane begin to move. "My child!" she screamed, "I must get my child!"

---

[2]Robert Hansen, from an article in *The Lutheran Standard*. Permission to quote given by Robert Hansen.

"Enemy bombers are closing in," the captain called back. "We can't delay. If we do, none of us will get off the ground alive." The plane picked up speed as it taxied down the runway. The mother ran to a window, and as the plane lifted and circled, she saw far below, standing alone on the runway, a tiny figure, gazing up with arms outstretched.

A Vietnamese friend described how it was for that mother the weeks they spent together at Camp Pendleton awaiting resettlement. "She was slowly going crazy," my friend said. "She would pace up and down, screaming and pulling her hair; then throwing herself down, she would bang her head against the ground. She had saved her suitcase with the bars of gold and jewels inside, but she had lost her child."

Of course, the Vietnamese mother did not intentionally leave her child behind. Nor do we intentionally neglect our children. But bereavement sometimes awakens us to the fact that this is actually happening, and our altered priorities can lead to enriched relationships which, in turn, bring new meaning to life.

Meaning in relationship with God

Reflecting on how our loss has affected our relationship to God can enrich us spiritually. Have we experienced more fully our need for the God who saves and forgives? Have we known in a new way His faithfulness, felt comforted by His understanding and been warmed by His love? Have words like "forgiveness," "acceptance," "courage," "patience," "endurance," "comfort," "fortitude," and "bravery" taken on new meaning? If such changes have taken place, then our loss has enriched us spiritually.

Reaching out to others

Two years after her 15-year-old son died of cancer, Vivian Johnson volunteered her services to the American Cancer Society to counsel parents of terminally ill children. "I found that helping others to survive aided my survival," Vivian said. "I believed my presence offered a living symbol of hope; I had experienced what they were experiencing and had survived. And not only had I survived, I was whole and happy once again. They could make it too!"

Marian and Don Balster, whose son died after he fell from his bike and struck his head on the pavement, have also brought a message of hope and comfort to hundreds. Together they founded an organization called Compassionate Friends and started a chapter, welcoming bereaved parents to their home. Gradually other chapters of the organization opened, and the network of Compassionate Friends continues to spread throughout the U.S.[3]

Making every day count

Orville E. Kelly, writing in *A.D.* magazine, said his life ended at 42 when he discovered he had cancer. It began again at 43 when he readjusted his life.

Kelly learned to accept each day as a day of life with which he had been blessed. But getting to this place didn't just happen. After the doctor told him that he had cancer, he and his wife, Wanda, unconsciously began to erect walls between themselves. They couldn't talk about the fact that he was dying.

Kelly wrote:

> One sunny afternoon I was driving back from a chemo-therapy treatment in Iowa City. Beautiful fields stretched out ahead of me. Just for a moment I forgot about the cancer that was eating away my life.
>
> Then I looked over at my wife beside me. I can't describe her look of sorrow and despair. It suddenly struck me how everything was falling apart because of me.
>
> I wasn't dead yet; I wasn't ready to die yet; I wasn't going to die yet. In fact, I felt pretty good that day. But I had been creating my own hell on earth.

---

[3] *The Compassionate Friends*, Nat'l. Headquarters, P.O. Box 1347, Oak Brook, Ill., 60521.

So I turned to my wife and said, "Wanda, let's talk about it." We had never really discussed the fact that I was dying. "Let's go home and tell the children. But then let's have some fun." We did. It wasn't easy, I will admit. But you know, that night I knew a joy, peace, and release I hadn't known for months.[4]

Not only did that honest, open facing of reality restore a close relationship between Kelly and his wife and children, but as a result, they were able to begin working together at making every day as beautiful as they could. And as they discovered that this was indeed possible, they began to share it with others. As a result, they founded an organization called *Make Today Count*, a support group for terminally ill patients.[5]

Perhaps Orville Kelly's words can offer us help as we seek to rediscover meaning in life:

Don't be afraid to die; don't be afraid to live. Do what you want to do. Pay for your mistakes, then start over. And happiness? How can you find it again? Go into your child's or your grandchild's bedroom, look at her face as she sleeps, bend down and kiss it. Go and have a conversation with a friend. Walk out in your yard, look up at the stars and pray. Ask yourself what you want out of life from now on. Thank God for all you have. Then perhaps happiness, as you call it, may begin to find you.[6]

Handling our grief

Some days, in spite of all our resolves, we may be tempted to ask, "Does it really make any difference how we allow our loss to affect us? Who cares, anyway?"

It does make a difference, and God cares. Others do also. The way in which we respond to loss may either push someone over the brink of despair into unbelief or it may light a candle

[4]Orville E. Kelly, *A.D.* magazine, January, 1975.
[5]*Make Today Count*, P.O. Box 222, Osage Beach, Mo., 65065. Telephone: (314) 348–1619.
[6]Kelly, op. cit.

of hope for them. The choices we make affect not only us but others.

High stakes and more

Hidden behind the scenes, a cosmic conflict goes on between God and Satan, a battle for our loyalty. Satan says as he did before Job's trials began: "Does Job fear God for nothing? . . . Stretch out your hand and strike everything he has, and he will surely curse you to your face" (Job 1:9, 11). Paul, in Romans 8:19, says that not only do bystanders wait to see how we will come through this testing, but all creation—trees, flowers, clouds, sun, rain, and the very grass we walk on—"waits in eager expectation for the sons of God to be revealed." Who, creation asks, will continue to trust in God when everything seems to have gone wrong?

Does it make any difference? Does anyone care? The answer to both is *yes!* God has given us freedom to choose and the power to affirm that life still has meaning and value.

Lord, take my hand and lead me
Upon life's way;
Direct, protect, and feed me
From day to day
Without your grace and favor
I go astray;
So take my hand, O Savior,
And lead the way.

Julie von Hausmann[7]

---

[7]Julie von Hausmann, "Lord, Take My Hand and Lead Me," from *Lutheran Book of Worship* (Minneapolis, Minn.: Augsburg Fortress, 1978). Copyright held by Augsburg Fortress and used by permission.

Somehow my heart can never learn to say
A last goodbye, entirely and completely,
To anything I ever loved. There may
Be folk who can accomplish severance neatly
With no loose ends of longing and regret
To trip their hearts at unexpected hours;
But always my heart stumbles, even yet,
When the shape of hills or the rain-sweet scent of
flowers
Recalls my earliest home, or when the sound
Of laughter echoes that which used to fall
From lips long silent to me. I am bound
By myriad threads of memory, keeping all
I ever loved so near me still, that I
Shall never learn to say a last goodbye.

—Jane Merchant[1]

[1]Jane Merchant, "Never a Last Goodbye," from *In Green Pastures* (Nashville, Tenn.: Abingdon Press). Copyright © 1959 held by Abingdon Press and used by permission.

Does Grieving Go on Forever?

*N*otes from my journal.

January 26

A friend said to me yesterday, "My mother died four years ago, and I still think of her almost every day." Wow! Why is the awareness of the person so much more constant for us after the person is dead than before?

August 17

It seems unbelievable. Seven months have passed, but not a day goes by without my thinking of Mother. Vague, unhappy, lonely feelings persist, sometimes making me lethargic.

Christmas Day

It's been a year since Mother's death, and I am in bed ill. Our first Christmas without dear Mother, and I have found myself often breaking down and weeping. Tip me the wrong way, and the tears spill over. The fact that I haven't been feeling well the past week hasn't helped. Today I feel rotten! I dragged myself to the Christmas Eve service last night. We had a beautiful poinsettia and white chrysanthemum bouquet on the altar in memory of Mother. Maybe that wasn't the best thing to do. It ripped open the old wound, and the service was very difficult for me.

March 1

Here more than a whole year has passed since Mother's death, and my thoughts still turn to her often.

April 23

On this day 27 years ago, our first little son was born and died. I wasn't thinking about it when I went to bed last night, but I dreamed. Our son had grown to young manhood and died, and I was engrossed in the burial service. We were laying his body to rest in a newly acquired piece of property that was going to be used for a cemetery, an area where the wilderness still claimed the land. We carried his casket down a path, stepping over shrubs, branches, and thorns that tore at us, feeling our way along. But most vivid of all was my profound sense of loss, grief, and sorrow—active, hurting suffering. I awakened weeping and feeling sore and bruised. Even now as I write these words, the tears flow. How deep are the wounds of separation which death inflicts! How grievous! What will it be like when we are finally healed? How incomplete our sense of wholeness must be in this life even though we sometimes think we feel healed and whole again.

Must grieving go on forever?

George H. Pollock, M.D., writing in the *International Journal of Psycho-Analysis*, says, "In the instance of the loss of a very significant object, the total mourning process may never be completed."

R. Scott Sullender believes that "as a general rule of thumb, the loss of a significant one requires a full year of grieving before one can be said to be fully 'recovered.' "[2]

I'm beginning to suspect that may be true. Conscious and fairly constant grieving need not go on forever, though it usually takes longer than we expect. But memories may always remain.

Glen W. Davidson, in his book *Understanding Mourning*, states that for an adult it seems to take between 18 and 24 months

---

[2]R. Scott Sullender, *Grief and Growth* (New Jersey: Paulist Press, 1985).

before signs of recovery become dominant.[3] That doesn't mean that periods of grieving won't continue, but they become fewer and farther apart.

Why recovery time varies

The length of time needed for recovery varies, in part, because people differ in how they perceive the magnitude of the loss. We usually endure a longer period of grief when a spouse, parent, or child has died than when a friend dies.

Personality will also affect the length of recovery. When President Reagan was dismissed from the hospital following his bout with cancer, the news photos showed him jaunty, waving and smiling—consistent with a man who takes time to chop wood and ride horses. We would have been shocked if we had seen him wailing and depressed.

Previous encounters with losses and the recovery we made also affect the present bereavement. Experience in grief may give us hope and peace in the midst of our crisis.

The length of grieving also depends on how "hard" we go at it, to what degree we suppress our grief or get it out in the open. If we face our loss openly and do not try to cover up our sorrow, we are likely to deal with grief more quickly.

If grieving is postponed, recovery may be delayed. Our work commitment may keep us so busy we do not have time to grieve. Or, we may have to conceal our grief at work. If we feel we've been grieving far too long, we may need to look back to see if we had the time or freedom to grieve fully when we first experienced the loss.

Following Mother's death I had a number of periods of illness that prolonged my recovery. The weakness that followed my illnesses introduced new temptations to doubt God's care for me, and if healing is to come, we must be assured of God's love for us. Our hope also is based on God's saving grace. *God*

---

[3]Glen W. Davidson, *Understanding Mourning* (Minneapolis, Minn.: Augsburg Publishing House, 1984).

will pull us through. If we think we can make it on our own, we may well find ourselves dangling on the edge of despair.

The process of grief

Time itself does not bring healing. In no way is that true! But time does allow us the space we need to work through our grief, for grief is a process.

Sometimes it is a confusing process. C. S. Lewis observed:

> In grief, nothing stays put. One keeps emerging from a phase, but it always recurs. Round and round. Everything repeats. Am I going in circles, or dare I hope I'm on a spiral? But if a spiral, am I going up or down it?[4]

The circling or spiraling is more noticeable at first. At times we may feel as if our gears have shifted to reverse and we are moving backwards. But the gears will eventually shift again into drive. After a while things will begin to straighten out, and we will find ourselves moving forward.

Recovery from grief does not mean we get over the emotional pain of our loss entirely. If it seems the wound finally has been covered with new tissue, we soon discover that the tissue is so thin and fragile that the slightest bump breaks it open, causing it to bleed again. But the pain is not as intense, the wound is not as deep, and the chances for infection not as great. In between bumps the wound may not hurt at all; in fact, we might not even think about it. The grief becomes a tempered grief, a calm grief.

"I can remember Stephen," my friend Leonore said ten years after her son's death, "with a feeling that resembles sorrow only as the mist resembles the rain."

If our relationship with our deceased one was a good one, thanksgiving and praise will accompany our grief—praise for the gift our loved one was to us, and praise to the Giver who gave our loved one to us. Our beloved's presence will remain

---

[4]C. S. Lewis, *A Grief Observed* (New York: Bantam Books, 1961).

with us, an aura of a gentle benediction.

So while time itself does not heal, time does play a part in healing grief—or rather, God, in time, heals grief, if we let Him. If the awful days of early grief were to continue endlessly, we could not bear to live; we surely could not function effectively, nor would we be able to move ahead.

Good grief

"Grief's purpose is to restore a person to health," Sullender pointed out. He writes:

> Grief is part of God's creation. . . . We can look upon grief, not as an enemy to be shunned, but as a friend to be welcomed. If allowed to do its work, uncontaminated by a repressive environment, grief will flow of its own accord— naturally and automatically—toward its final goal of restored health."[5]

Signs of recovery

How do we know when healing has taken place to a healthy degree?

- We don't think about our deceased loved one as much as we did before.
- We begin to make plans for the future.
- We begin to feel energetic again, able to care for the daily things that call for our attention.
- We aren't making as many foolish decisions as we did for a while.
- We have returned to regular eating patterns, and we are sleeping better.
- If we are a bereaved spouse, we aren't letting others (usually our children) make all our decisions for us. We make them ourselves.
- We aren't dwelling so much on the "what ifs" or wor-

---

[5]Sullender, op. cit.

rying our hearts out over what might never happen.
- We are beginning to discover who we are as a person, not just as a role-filler.
- We feel free to laugh and have a good time.

If grief is still overwhelming us, we may take heart. Things will get better. God, who walks beside us, says,

I am the Lord your God,
who takes hold of your right hand
and says to you,
Do not fear; I will help you.
Fear not, for I have redeemed you;
I have summoned you by name; you are mine.
When you pass through the rivers,
they will not sweep over you.
When you walk through the fire,
you will not be burned;
the flames will not set you ablaze.
For I am the Lord, your God,
the Holy One of Israel, your Savior.

Isaiah 41:13; 43:1–3

Into the morning a small bird came winging
Up to the cherry bough whitening my door,
Out of his flute-throat his wild pulse was flinging
Notes he had learned from an unwritten score.

Roused from my sleep, I turned on my pillow
Away from the shadow belonging to night,
Watching the bird ride the blossoming billow
As breezes kept rolling him into my sight.

If in the dark there is kept for our keeping
A lark or a longspur to bring in the dawn,
So may it be in a far longer sleeping
There'll be a small bird to wake us with song.

Ralph W. Seager[1]

---

[1]Ralph W. Seager, "Into the Morning," from *Wheatfields and Vineyards* (New York: Christian Herald). Copyright held by Ralph W. Seager and used by permission.

Life After Death

As the months after Mother's death passed and healing began to take place, I was better able to take to myself the comfort Scripture offered.

"Where is Mother now?" had been one of the questions that had tortured me as I had looked at Mother's lifeless body. I discovered an answer to that question in a roundabout way.

The account of Jesus' transfiguration on the mount and His conversation with Elijah and Moses fascinated me as I read it. Unique circumstances had surrounded the final days on earth of Moses and Elijah. God himself had buried Moses. Elijah had been caught up to heaven in a chariot of fire.

In the transfiguration scene, both Moses and Elijah appeared to be in possession of new or transformed bodies, for the disciples saw and recognized both of them. Moses and Elijah evidently also had minds that could think and voices that could talk (Matt. 17:3).

I began to wonder what had taken place for these two during the centuries that had passed after they had died but before they reappeared on the mount. Did they know Christ before the Incarnation? Had they talked with Him, "the Lamb slain from the foundation of the world," about the Father's plan to woo back to himself His wayward children by sending His Son to earth? Even as I asked myself these questions I realized I was speaking from an earthly point of view and that perhaps speculation was foolish. But still the questions were there.

I shifted my attention from the disciples to Christ as He appeared on the mount. He was transfigured: His immortality dominated His mortality; His deity superceded His humanity. And as Jesus was visible in this godly form, Moses, Elijah, and Jesus talked about the Lord's coming death.

Did Moses and Elijah reappear on the mount to remind, reassure, and strengthen Christ? If so, what wonder that these two former earth-children could impart strength, reassurance, and courage to the Son of God!

Peter couldn't understand it at all. Completely befuddled, he wanted to construct three booths, thus elevating Moses and Elijah to a position equal with Christ.

But while Peter was speaking, the cloud overshadowed them, and the curtain was dropped. Peter couldn't respond appropriately to insight into life after death, so God spoke out of the cloud, "Look to Jesus, Peter. He is my beloved Son. Listen to what He says to you."

Peter never forgot that day. He was still left with unanswered questions, but he was absolutely sure of one thing: Jesus had power, majesty, honor, and glory from God the Father. So if Jesus said, "When I die, I will overcome death, the enemy, and pull from death's mouth the tongue that can sting and poison and kill forever," Peter was ready to believe Christ. If Jesus said, "As surely as I leave you and you will see me no more, just as surely I will return to take you to myself," Peter was ready to believe Him.

Having seen the curtain pulled aside briefly on the Mount of Transfiguration gave Peter a glimpse of glory that later developed into an indomitable faith, a faith so secure Peter was willing to give his life for it.

"But," I protested, during my early days of bereavement, "there is no mount for me."

Do you need one? the answer seemed to come back. *Look to Jesus.*

As I did, I noticed how little Jesus spoke about life after death to his disciples; yet one truth stood out: over and over Jesus declared that after we die, *we shall be with Him.* To the thief on the cross, He said, "Today *you shall be with me.*" To His disciples Jesus said, "I will come back and take you *to be with me, that you also may be where I am*" (John 14:3). "Father, I want those you have given me *to be with me where I am,*" Jesus prayed (John 17:24). "Whoever serves me must follow me, and *where I am, my servant also will be*" (John 12:26).

No sooner are we "absent from the body" than we are "present with the Lord." The transition is immediate and conscious. G. H. Knight says:

> There is not for the dying believer (as many imagine and many say) a long interval of unconsciousness between death and the resurrection. Paul speaks of 'them that sleep,' but it is the body, not the soul, that sleeps. In the sleep of the body even here, dreams show that the soul is thoroughly awake, though concerned with a different region than its surrounding one; and the expression 'sleeping' as applied to the dead is merely a figurative one, implying peace and rest, but not implying anything like unconsciousness. Indeed the idea that the soul continues in a state of virtual annihilation all the time that Christ is waiting for His kingdom is not only unscriptural but unthinkable. If it is 'with Christ' in any real sense, it must be conscious that it is, and must know and feel what that fellowship means.[2]

The Bible does not clearly state what form or nature our life takes during the interval before our souls are united with bodies. We know that even on this earth life takes many forms. A fetus has life, a far different life from life after birth. We continue to live while we sleep, but our dream life is different from our waking hours. We may anticipate that being with the Lord in the consciousness we shall possess after death will be different from any definition of life we have known before.

Even the great apostle Paul experienced some tension as he

---

[2]G. H. Knight, *In the Cloudy and Dark Day* (Rock Island, Ill.: Augustana Book Concern, 1934).

thought about this. He was sure, he wrote, that "a building from God, a house not made with hands" awaited him in heaven. But he was not sure when he would be clothed with that new body. He did not as much fear being "unclothed," that is, having this earthly body die and decay, as he felt uneasy not knowing how long he might have to remain "unclothed," that is, be spirit without body. He said he "groaned," longing to put on his eternal body so he wouldn't be found naked. He sighed with anxiety as he thought about it, yet he exhibited courage, being willing to walk by faith, to trust God through it all (2 Cor. 5:1–7).

How conscious will we be of time after we die? I wondered. *Will the period between "being with the Lord" and the period of receiving our new bodies seem endless?* Luther comments:

> Before God, a thousand years are scarcely a day, and when the resurrection comes, it will seem to Adam and the old fathers as though they had been alive only half an hour before.[3]

Luther compared the interval of waiting to falling sleep. It is impossible for us to know the hour and minute we fall asleep. And often when we awaken, we feel as though we had just fallen asleep though hours may have passed.

Knowing that we shall "be with Christ" should be sufficient. And is it not enough for us as mourners to think of our deceased loved ones as being presented faultless in the presence of our Lord with joy? Would we want them back on earth again?

C. S. Lewis, writing about his immense sorrow after his wife died, ended his memoirs in his little book *A Grief Observed* with these words:

> How wicked it would be, if we could, to call the dead back! She said not to me but to the chaplain, "I am at peace with God." She smiled, but not at me.[4]

Resurrection day shall come. We cannot stretch our imagi-

---

[3]Martin Luther, *What Luther Says*, Compiled by Edward M. Plass (St. Louis, Mo.: Concordia Publishing House, 1987).
[4]C. S. Lewis, *A Grief Observed* (New York: Bantam Books Inc., 1961).

nations far enough to understand the degree of vitality and life we shall possess when our spirits are united with our resurrected bodies. The new body will possess new qualities. Revelation 21:4 tells us we will be free of suffering, hunger, thirst, disease, pain, and death. The resurrected body will possess a glory and brilliance difficult for us to comprehend now (1 Cor. 15:43; Dan. 12:3; 2 Cor. 3:18; Matt. 17:2). Powers that are imperfect now will be perfect then. "The body will have sharp eyes," Luther wrote, "so as to be able to see through a mountain, and quick ears, so as to be able to hear from one end of the earth to the other."[5]

The Bible has nothing to say about our "age" when we are resurrected, possibly because time and age, as we know them in this world, will be so vastly different in the world to come.

Will we know each other? Although we have no clear-cut statement in Scripture, it seems incredible that we would not. However, most significant will be that we shall know God more fully than ever, for we shall know Him "face to face" (Matt. 5:8; John 17:24; 1 John 3:2). The psalmist anticipated that meeting with joy. "I—in righteousness I will see your face," he declared with assurance. "When I awake, I will be satisfied with seeing your likeness" (Ps. 17:15).

We also shall see fully the fruits of our service to Christ. "They will rest from their labor, for their deeds follow them" (Rev. 14:13). And we shall stand "blameless" before God (Rev. 14:5).

Thus, as the months passed after Mother's death, I found my soul quickened again to a living hope. Faith grew stronger. When my sister Alma died, I was able to stand by her bedside, weeping, but untroubled. And as Thyra and I stood outside watching the silver balloon soaring higher and higher into the black, star-studded heavens, it had seemed a symbol to me that Alma indeed, now absent to us, was home with the Lord. I was able to gather that comfort close to myself and feel the warmth of God's presence and love with me. God's Word had fanned a smoldering faith to a bright flame.

---

[5]Luther, op. cit.

Epilogue

Reaching back from here
All that I remember of my life
Are the great round rocks and not
The unimportant stones.
I know that I have experienced pain, and yet
The scars have healed so that
I am like the tree covering itself
With new growth every year.
I know that I have walked in sadness, and yet
All that I remember now
Is the soothing autumn light.
I know that there was much to make my life
unhappy
If I had stopped to notice how
The world sings a broken song.
But I preferred to dwell within
A universe of fields and streams
Which echoed the wholeness of my song.

Nancy Wood[1]

---

[1]Nancy Wood, "Looking Back from Here" from *Many Winters* by Nancy Wood (New York: Doubleday). Copyright 1974.